Skyhorse Publishing books may be purchased in bulk at special discounts for sales promotion, corporate gifts, fund-raising, or educational purposes. Special editions can also be created to specifications. For details, contact the Special Sales Department, Skyhorse Publishing, 307 West 36th Street, 11th Floor, New York, NY 10018 or info@skyhorsepublishing.com.

Skyhorse® and Skyhorse Publishing® are registered trademarks of Skyhorse Publishing, Inc.®, a Delaware corporation.

Visit our website at www.skyhorsepublishing.com.

10 9 8 7 6 5 4 3 2 1

Library of Congress Cataloging-in-Publication Data is available on file.

Cover design by Rain Saukus

Print ISBN: 978-1-63220-722-7
Ebook ISBN: 978-1-63220-841-5

Printed in China

madewithdad

From Wizards' Wands to Japanese Dolls, Craft Projects to Build, Make, and Do with Your Kids

Chris Barnardo

Skyhorse Publishing

To India, James, William, and Albie
with all my love, Dad xxx

bottle-cap beetle PAGE 29

contents

For printable designs and templates to enhance your madewithdad projects, visit our dedicated website at:

www.madewithdad.com

Introduction

In 2005, I started writing a blog called dadcando aimed at helping dads get the most out of the time they spend with their children. The idea was to lend dads a hand on a practical level by sharing some of my experiences, and to be a positive celebration of a father's role in his child's life while providing a creative resource for both dads and their children. It was a call to dads to celebrate their abilities and help them realize how important the things they do are in turning their children into happy and successful adults. Research has shown that a father's role, and specifically the quality and sensitivity of play between a father and his children, is the most important factor in determining a growing child's ability to form and maintain normal relationships and feel secure in themselves(1). So, because of the importance of play, I built my blog around a core of original creative craft projects that I knew would engage children while tapping into a father's inner child. *Made with Dad* builds on the success of *dadcando*. *Made with Dad*'s goal of enriching the relationship between father and child is relevant to any busy dad who feels that he would like to get more out of the precious moments he spends with his children. *Made with Dad* revolves around an adventure into the creative mind of the child and awakens the child in the heart of every dad.

For the dad and his child, *Made with Dad*'s craft and model-making projects provide a focus for time spent together, and the finished item sticks around as a constant reminder of good times spent together with a toy that will give hours of entertainment. *Made with Dad* projects enable a dad to spend quality time with his kids, and by keeping his eyes and ears open, he gets to fundamentally understand how his children think and feel in a way that can't be beat.

Making things together goes much further than the immediate satisfaction of the finished model. The lessons that are learned by solving all the problems that building something from scratch translates extremely well into everyday life.

Problem solving is an important life skill, and in my view, the key to happiness. *Made with Dad* teaches this in a very subtle way. Each craft project provides the perfect opportunity for practicing problem-solving skills in a safe environment, which will have a hugely beneficial effect on how projecteers perceive and then tackle the bigger challenges in their lives. The projects are designed to appeal to children and parents alike by developing both fathers' and children's natural skills. The clear project plans don't diminish the need for creativity or problem solving on the part of the dad and child, because everyone's starting materials are slightly different and many small issues must be creatively solved if the task is to be completed. The plans form an outline of the tried-and-true route for any given project from start to finish, making each one manageable and acting as a framework to give the novice builders confidence to tackle projects that they might otherwise never try.

Developing our creativity is important because it is the engine that powers our problem-solving ability. Creativity is not an innate gift that only a lucky few have; we are all born with it. Tapping back into our intrinsic creativity is a skill anyone can master.

Becoming creative is a two-step process. The first step is simply to start seeing the world differently from how you have learned to see it. Some may argue that creativity is actually seeing the world as it really is, not just how we *think* it is. Once you can see the world as it really is, you become able to see all the options available to you, and you can put them together in new and exciting ways—this is the second part of the creative process. This

William's pompom

is why creativity is key to problem solving. It's what lets you break out of the trap of going over the same solution time and again, thinking that in doing so you might make it work even though you have failed that way one hundred times before.

It's obvious, really, in order to find new solutions to old problems, you have to think new thoughts. Creative people call thinking new thoughts, "thinking outside-the-box." The box is the imaginary container that constrains our thinking and makes sure we always go down the same well-trodden path. The box is what stops us thinking new thoughts and trying new ways of doing things. It's what causes us to make the same mistakes over and over again. Our parents helped us build our box during our upbringing, and as we've grown up, we have reinforced it to a bulletproof thickness with habits and surroundings that we don't see anymore. It's the ceiling that stops us from soaring. It is the box that we are building for our children that will surely turn them into us.

Thinking outside the box is not difficult, but you have to work at it, because the box has created an almost impenetrable barrier around our free thinking. Sometimes it is difficult to know where to start, and it is hard to know when we are actually thinking outside-the-box. My "Bucket Thought Experiment" illustrates the problem and its solution beautifully. Ask anyone to come up with as many uses for a bucket as they can. Tell them that you're aiming for twenty-five different ways of using a bucket. Typically, you will get answers like: something to carry water in, a coal bucket, an ice bucket, or a vase. At first glance, it looks like a good start, but all of these uses are the same—a container. To think outside-the-box,

India's pelican sketch

you have to come up with *different* uses for the bucket. Some examples of different uses might be: a megaphone (knock the bottom out); a small stepladder; a hat; a sandcastle maker; a weapon; or an *objet d'art*.

Kids naturally do this sort of thing all the time, and as we relearn how to think like this for ourselves, we not only start to see new ways of getting around old problems, but we also start to understand our children so much better. Once you can look at a bottle top and see a pair of dragon hunter's goggles, or hold a toothbrush and imagine a fighter-

James' peg chameleon

plane wingtip, then you are starting to get the idea. You will find that this fresh way of thinking brings out the positive aspects of the child inside you, has a dramatic effect on the way you think about lots of things, and most importantly of all, helps you get the most out of the time you spend with your kids.

Children don't need much to set their imaginations on fire, and are desperate to participate in the fictional universes of their favorite game and story characters. The chapter called "Great Adventures" plays to this need by adding stories to each project, turning those projects into imaginary voyages of discovery, and providing a starting point for the richest possible interaction with each craft activity.

Here's to new and happy times, *Made With Dad*.

Albie's submarine

1. Grossmann, *et al*, The Uniqueness of the Child-Father Attachment Relationship: Fathers' Sensitive and Challenging Play as a Pivotal Variable in a 16-year Longitudinal Study, Social Development, Volume 11, Number 3, July 2002, pp. 301–337(37), Blackwell Publishing.

Having the right stuff

In this book, you'll discover loads of exciting making and doing projects. For some, you'll only need five minutes; with others, whole afternoons will dissolve away. Some require just a piece of paper, while for others, you'll need old packaging junk and a few bits of basic making equipment. Some models are easy to put together; whereas others will help you and your children develop more advanced scratch-building skills.

Whichever projects you choose, you'll find that the instructions have been carefully designed to be very clear, and the finished product is cheap to make. For the most part, the bits you'll need to make the model cost nothing, or are free bits of garbage that you would normally throw away!

The projects here are completely original, fun and relevant to kids, and have been designed with you in mind. Quick and easy with really satisfying results, they ensure that even when time is short you can get the most out of the moments you and your children have together. Making and doing things with your kids is about giving them the most valuable thing you can give them—your time. Our 'with' projects are about solving problems together and having something at the end that your child can keep, play with, and feel proud of. Anything you make with your children will be very special to them because you spent the time together making it.

Most of the instructions come with templates or patterns that you can trace over to ensure that all the models you make look as good as they possibly can. But before you start, here's some information and advice on the tools and equipment you will need for the more involved projects.

CUT IT

Craft knives

While scissors are much safer, and you should use those when you can, there will come a time when you have to use a knife to cut something out. We are assuming that you know how to use a knife carefully. Most model makers have a few 'width' from slips made with very sharp knives when they were rushing, tired, or not paying attention. However, if you are careful, cutting something out with the right knife will give you a very good finish.

Always use the right knife for the job

Craft knives come in a wide range of different shapes and sizes, but the most useful are the Stanley knife and the scalpel. For jobs that don't require fine detail and are

too tough for a scalpel, the utility or box-cutter knife (commonly known as a Stanley knife, after the company that first manufactured it in volume) is very handy. The smaller craft knife, which has a long blade that can be snapped off at intervals to keep it sharp, is also useful, but if you have a Stanley knife and a scalpel then you have most things covered. The design of most craft knives allows the blade to be retractable for safe storage, but even so, these pieces of equipment should always be stored somewhere out of the reach of your children.

Sharp knives should never be used by children, and you should be careful when using them. You can teach your kids a great deal about responsible use of equipment by setting a good example when you use a knife to cut out something for them.

SAFETY FIRST

A Stanley knife will make short work of most forms of packaging, and the vase project on page 20 was made in about twenty minutes just by slicing up a couple of empty plastic bottles.

When planning what to cut, it's best to draw on the surface using a thin permanent marker so that you can make a neat incision in the right place. To draw a straight line around the base of a bottle, hold it with the end to be cut in the palm of the hand you write with, while holding the marker. Press the marker against the bottle where you want to cut it and draw around the bottle by revolving it without moving the pen. That way you will get a nice horizontal line. Take care when cutting the necks of bottles, as these are the thickest parts and are often impossible to cut with any knife. The best way to cut through the neck of a plastic bottle is with a junior hacksaw. Using a junior hacksaw is safe for kids because the saw teeth are very small, and it's a fun way to teach them how to use a saw.

Scalpel

The scalpel deserves a special mention here because it is the cutting tool of choice for the graphics and model-making industry. Typically, craft knives are differentiated from other knives because they have removable, disposable blades that allow you to keep them as sharp as possible. There are a huge number of differently shaped blades and handles available, so it is easy to get confused, but it does make the scalpel one of the most flexible knives.

Each blade type has a number, as does each handle

A very sharp knife, traditionally used by surgeons, that's great for cutting out detail in relatively thin materials

variant. For model making, you only need one blade shape, and that's number 10A. (Note: do not get a number 10, as this type has a curved blade edge and is very difficult – dangerous even – to cut with against a ruler.) The handle variant to go for is handle number 3. Change the blade regularly so that it stays sharp and you don't have to press too hard when cutting. If the material you are working with is thick or tough, then use a stronger craft knife rather than risk pressing so firmly that you snap the scalpel blade. The blades are sold singly, in little foil packs of 5, or in boxes of 100. However, a box of 100 bought online only costs twice as much as a pack of 5 bought in my local art shop, so as with anything, it is most definitely worth buying in bulk.

Scalpel blades are extremely sharp and are perfect for cutting foamboard, thin cardboard, or paper so that the edges are really neat. As with any blade, scalpels should be handled with care and children should never be allowed to use them. That is definitely a job for Dad or Mom. Be careful when changing the blade because it is easy to slip, and take care when model making. Always put the tool out of the reach of your children when using it, and after use, remove the blade and put it back in its packaging so that it doesn't jab you when you're rummaging around in the kitchen drawer later on.

SAFETY FIRST

TIP: Because of its very fine point, a scalpel is perfect for cutting round, small details. But remember, the blade is so sharp that it will cut through more than just the layer you want to cut, so always work on a surface where it won't matter if it gets marked.

Any piece of thick cardboard will do for a makeshift cutting mat, and most graphic designers resort to using the back of their drawing pads in an emergency. However, a self-healing cutting mat is probably a wise investment; it extends the life of your blades, makes cutting more controllable (it slows the blade down as you cut with it), and will save you making horrendous marks and scratches in your kitchen tabletop.

MODEL IT

Foamboard

Also called polyboard or foamcore, foamboard is a wonderfully light, yet rigid, cardboard 3 mm to 5 mm thick, made from sandwiching a layer of Styrofoam between two sheets of thin, high-quality cardboard. It's really easy to cut and folds to give clean, professional-looking bends.

The glue gun works a treat on foamboard, so you can quickly knock together some impressive models with it. It is a very rewarding material to use because finished models are robust and the excellent surface will take a range of paint finishes, from markers to emulsion and spray paint. Kids love this board and it's great for creating something special for homework or to take into school. The most useful size to go for is probably 5 mm thick, A2, which will cover you for practically every project.

> **A fabulous material for making structural models very quickly, it's lightweight and bends and cuts beautifully**

To bend foamboard, cut a V-shaped groove in one side, being careful not to cut all the way through, and then fold. If you want a really strong fold, run a line of glue-gun glue along the bottom of the V-shaped groove before bending it into shape.

Of course you shouldn't write off other types of board. We are bombarded with packaging these days, and it is generally made from a wide range of engineering-quality materials. The sides of plastic washing-powder bottles are thin sheets of polyethylene (PE) or polypropylene (PP), and fruit juice cartons are usually waxed or PE-coated and foil-lined, medium-weight, cardboard – cut one open and look inside. These materials look great when used on a model.

For small, flexible sheets try cutting open an old toothpaste tube; many of them are made from multilayer barrier plastics with a foil lining, and that's magic stuff for putting the finishing touches to a range of great models.

Different types of cardboard

Thin, lightweight card from breakfast cereal packaging or a craft shop is useful for small models and surface finishing touches. It can be bent and cut easily with scissors.

Thick pulp board is the kind you find on the back of a sketching pad. Good strength, but difficult to cut or bend. You will need a craft knife and to be very careful when cutting.

Corrugated or fluted packing board is readily available at your local supermarket, where they throw away tons of cardboard boxes. It can be strong, bends well one way (along the flutes), and is reasonably easy to cut using a knife or strong scissors. It also glues well with a glue gun.

Medium-thickness foamboard is quite expensive at about $3 (do a web search for the cheapest and buy it online) and you will need sharp knives for cutting it, but this board cuts, folds, and glues with a glue gun very nicely. It can be difficult to get radius bends, though.

Polymorph

I stumbled across Polymorph in the Maplin catalogue and thought it might come in handy for something or other. Composed of plastic chips that soften in hot water at about 140°F, it can be molded by hand before setting rock hard, so it's great for molding small components like robot hands, doll or puppet faces, or dolls' house items, for example. It's a plastic with a very low melting point that sets as tough as polypropylene and is almost indestructible when it's set. A useful quantity (250 g) in granule form, only costs about $12, and when you want to use it, you just put the granules in a jug and pour boiling water over them.

> A hot-water softening plastic that sets rock hard in minutes, great for molding little details for your models

After about two minutes in the hot water, the granules, which start out opaque white, go transparent and start to agglomerate and soften. Once it's transparent, you pour the water away—none of it gets absorbed and the lump of plastic can be taken from the jug and molded into any shape you like. When hot, Polymorph is very malleable, and yet it is just about cool enough to manipulate with your bare hands. However, younger children should not be allowed to handle the hot plastic, and young people of 12 years and over will still need some supervision.

The hot plastic is easy to form and holds its shape reasonably well while it is setting. However, it is not an ideal modeling clay because there is a degree of elasticity to its behavior, rather than it being perfectly plastic. Nevertheless, the brilliant thing about Polymorph is that within a few minutes, as it cools, it quickly hardens into a very tough, rigid white plastic that is

* the revolutionary plastic that melts in hot water
* just heat up and mould by hand
* hardens as it cools – strong as nylon
* 101 uses for DIY and model making

completely reusable. If you are not happy with the result, simply return it to the hot water and it softens again.

The product specification and instructions claim that you can machine the hardened plastic, but I would beg to differ on this point. The average person's home-machining tools are not water cooled, and so typical equipment like electric drills and jigsaws will generate so much heat from friction that the material rapidly goes over its softening point, and it therefore becomes impossible to get a good finish. In addition to that, it's far too tough to carve with a knife when it is set. In fact, attempting to do so could be very dangerous if the piece is not held down properly because it is very slippery. My advice is to use Polymorph to make selected components within your model and aim to make them entirely by molding them in the few minutes of soft time you have after you have heated the material. Once you are happy with the result, the hardened material can be colored in using permanent markers, or painted with acrylic or spray paint.

STICK IT

Double-sided sticky tape

There are loads of different types of sticky tape available, but when model making or doing crafts, none is quite as useful as double-sided sticky tape. Double-sided sticky tape is a very thin plastic tape coated with an open adhesive on both sides and is supplied rolled up and stuck on to a nonstick release paper. It provides very quick, clean, and relatively strong sticking power for cardboard, paper, and board. Children can use it without getting into a gluey mess and the results are very neat.

Cut small squares of tape and use them as little sticky pads for holding paper in place in frames or when folded up. Stick it to the back of things before you cut them out so that you make sure you have edge-to-edge adhesive. Use it in place of wet glue or a glue stick to make envelopes for a really strong finish.

> **One of the best ways to stick paper and cardboard together strongly and neatly with no mess**

Double-sided sticky tape is great for wrapping presents up neatly because you put the tape on the underside of the paper and don't spoil the wrapping paper you've used.

Get your children to draw their own stickers and then put double-sided tape on the back of the paper and cut the stickers out with a pair of kitchen scissors. They can then peel off the backing whenever they want and use the stickers they've made.

Wet glues

There are a range of glues available for use in the home. Polyvinyl acetate or PVA glue (also referred to as white glue or wood glue) is a tough, rubbery polymer. Your kids will be familiar with PVA because it is used extensively in schools. From a model-making point of view, nothing is a substitute for the power and speed of a glue gun—so in my house, the PVA glue tends to stay in the cupboard. Nevertheless, it's still a superb wood glue, where the water-based glue vehicle can really wet out the surface and soak into the wood to create a joint that is often

Choose the right glue for the right job, otherwise you will waste a lot of time waiting for things to dry

stronger than the surrounding wood. The trouble with PVA is that it is not good at sticking polythene or polypropylene, which are the two most common packaging plastics, and materials that are used in quite a few of the models in this book. It also takes ages to dry, which means that kids can lose interest in the project or have to wait overnight to see the results of their handiwork.

However, PVA works brilliantly for papier-mâché projects. Just water it down a bit, no more than half glue and half water, and pour the glue onto a dinner plate so the paper can be soaked through more easily. A mixture of newspaper and absorbent kitchen paper towels torn into strips or crumpled up into balls provides quick bulk for papier-mâché.

Doing a project like this will be great fun and very messy, so although most PVAs are washable, your kids shouldn't be in their Sunday best when they are getting glue all over themselves. Don't bother buying tiny little bottles of PVA; go to a hardware store and buy a 2.5 liter bottle of PVA Bonding. It's basically exactly the same as the expensive wood glue, but it's a fraction of the price. If you want a handy pack to use around the house or on little paper projects, just decant some of it into an old shampoo bottle, but remember to write on the bottle what it is in permanent marker or someone who doesn't know what you've done could be heading for one gloopy hairdo!

Glue sticks and two-part resins are OK but not as useful as

Spray Mount and a glue gun, which, respectively, replace them. Glue sticks tend to be lumpy, although they do have the advantage of being easy and safe for a child to use. Two-part resins are very strong, but they take time to cure, can be very messy, and do not stick packaging plastics together that well. Once they are mixed, they are very liquid, and for many jobs, you might have trouble keeping the glue exactly where you want it. For just about every model-making project where a two-part resin could be used, glue-gun glue will work better and is easier to use.

Superglue (cyanoacrylate) is very good at sticking skin together – there are medical grades approved for closing wounds – and great care must be taken when using it. Children should never be allowed to use superglue. It sticks vinyl (PVC) together very well, so is useful for mending most types of blow-up beach toys (use an old vinyl tax disc holder or window sticker as the patch), but is not suitable for most model- and toy-making projects because it is so thin, and it's designed to stick broken surfaces together only when they match perfectly.

SAFETY FIRST

Spray glue

Spray glue (also called by its leading brand name, Spray Mount) is what started me thinking about the availability of performance glues and proper 'making stuff' for kids to use, just like grown-ups. In the graphics industry, Spray Mount replaced Cow Gum as a rapid-fix glue for sticking sheet materials together.

Once you have used spray glue, you are unlikely to ever go back to any other form of wet glue for sticking sheets of paper or cardboard together. A light dusting is all that's needed to fix things like photos in place, and, yes, it's the glue they use in those kids' TV shows when they've finished a picture and magically place it on a background where it stays. No wrinkling up at the edges, no wet patches, and if you stick your picture down in the wrong place or slightly askew, then on most surfaces it is repositionable for the first few minutes.

Simply the best way to stick sheets of paper or cardboard to each other

As with any aerosol, kids should not be allowed to use this glue unsupervised. Remember, as it's a spray, the glue will get everywhere. When you use it, make sure you read the instructions and only do so in a ventilated room. Spray on to a surface that you don't mind getting glue on – usually that means putting down loads of newspaper, even more than you would think!

SAFETY FIRST

There is a knack to using this adhesive though, and if you are not careful, you can end up covering other things with oversprayed glue. This can be a problem, as it is very sticky and hard to remove without using an artist's alcohol based cleaning solvent. Your best bet is to lay the piece to be covered in glue upside-down in the middle of a large piece of old newspaper and make sure you don't spray onto the surrounding area.

We use spray glue to stick all manner of templates and printed paper to anything flat that needs decorating. It is ideal for sticking things like photos, tickets, and news clippings neatly into a scrapbook.

Glue gun

No home is complete without a glue gun. Yes, it sounds like a bold statement. You may also think it a bit excessive of me to claim that it is one of the best inventions of the twentieth century, if not of all time. I know that the best invention was the printing press, but the glue gun has the power to unlock your children's imagination and allow you and them to make things out of old junk as quickly as you want. Who knows how many future inventors, entrepreneurs, and professors were set on the road to greatness by something as humble as the glue gun?

So, what is it? The glue gun is a device for melting a thermoplastic resin glue, usually in the form of a long, milky-colored stick about 1 cm in diameter. The glue is extremely tough when set, and because it typically takes less than a minute to harden, it is perfect for instantaneous, high-performance sticking when making things. In fact, I would say that if you have a glue gun, permanent marker, and some old discarded packaging, you have almost everything you need to start making something good right away.

There are both low- and high-temperature versions of the glue gun, but

One of the greatest inventions ever, and you can buy one for around $12!

as even the low-temperature ones can reach 100°C and cause nasty burns, so care should be taken when using either type. Children should be supervised at all times, even if they have used them before.

The great thing about a glue gun when making things is that it will stick almost any object or surface to any other and can even be used to backfill cracks and gaps.

A glue gun will only cost about $12 and can be bought online or in any DIY store. Once you have one, you'll find that its usefulness extends far beyond these projects into fixing all manner of things around the home. I'd recommend that you get an extra packet of sticks when you buy your glue gun as they can get used up quite quickly.

SAFETY FIRST I know I keep saying it, but . . . glue guns and melted glue get very hot indeed and the glue is also very sticky. Children should not be allowed to use a glue gun unsupervised, and if they are using it under supervision, they need to be shown which bits heat up and learn how to use the gun without getting the hot melted glue on their fingers. If a burn does occur, get the glue off the skin as quickly as possible and run the burned area under cold water for at least five minutes. Turn your glue gun off after using it and put it to the back of the work surface out of reach while it cools down. Make sure the wire isn't trailing anywhere where it might get tripped over.

COLOR IT

Paint

You don't have to use paint to finish off your models, but it can make a big difference to the overall look.

Not all models really need paint, but items made from objects with writing or labels on them will look about a million times better if the lettering is covered up. In the case of the *Space Rocket* (p. 162), we used white paper wrapped around a chip tube and a toilet paper roll to give us the nice white finish, which we could then use marker on without getting our fingers wet. For the *Floating Submarine* (p. 95), black- and-gray spray paint transformed it in about two minutes from a couple of old plastic bottles into something really exciting that remained a favorite bathtime toy for months.

Use spray paint or emulsion for a quick finish that covers almost anything really well

You can use any type of spray paint, but be careful to follow the instructions on the can. The paint is flammable when being sprayed, is bad for you if you breathe in the fumes, and leaves a strong smell in your house for days. On the other hand, spray paint is ideal for quickly and permanently covering plastic, and spray paint for craft applications comes in a range of exciting finishes.

For quick coverage on most surfaces, you can do a lot worse than standard, house-decorating emulsion. If you don't have any left over from your own DIY projects, then you can buy tiny cans of paint, also known as match pots, very cheaply. Emulsion is better for covering cardboard quickly and the beauty of it is that you can wash the brushes in water. Be careful of clothes, though; emulsion dries in about two minutes and thereafter is impossible to remove.

canoe PAGE 107

Acrylic paint is also very good at covering lettering up and sticking to most surfaces, and although it is water based, it has the benefit of being permanent—rather than water soluble—when it's dry. Acrylic paints dry very quickly and give bright satisfying colors, and they can also be used to tint emulsion. Tubes of acrylic are reasonably expensive, but they are lovely to use and the colors in them can all be mixed together to give a very professional finish. Acrylic paint also comes in big bottles that are much cheaper and can be picked up at most good toy shops or online.

Permanent markers

Surface decoration really makes a difference to the look of your models. You can paint them with emulsion or spray, but a very quick way to finish them off is by drawing on them with a permanent marker. Permanent markers can stain, so be careful with your clothes.

A very quick way to let your kids personalize your models, giving them detail and character

The best marker to have for most uses is the bulletpoint type, like the medium one shown here. It's also useful to have a thinner one—the type of marker you use to write on CDs or overhead projector film is ideal. And of course, because you want things to be fun, why not get a huge jumbo marker? They're not expensive and the kids always have fun coloring in using such a big pen and loads of black ink! Markers are perfect for adding names and little details to models that you have sprayed or painted over all in one color. Always write something on your models; it is an important finishing step. Let your kids name the model or think up and design imaginary organizations and logos. If the model needs a number, then why not use a number special to them, their age or their favorite number? Play is all about buying into the fantasy, and these finishing touches and little ways of personalizing your homemade model add a huge

amount of play. Don't forget that permanent markers now come in gold and silver and can be used to color a whole range of cardboards and plastics to instantly a bright, metallic finish.

Before you actually put pen to model, type out what you want to write on your model using your computer. Type at the right size and use a font style that you like or is particularly suitable—the NASA font for spaceships or a stencil font for hardware, for example. Then, using the typed letters as a reference, copy the text on to the model using the marker. You could also look for reference images of real versions of your model and copy their sponsorship and logos—you'll be surprised at the difference a few carefully placed graphics will make.

The canoe (opposite page) only took about 30 minutes to make. It's not painted, but it is completely transformed by the name drawn onto it.

ILLUMINATE IT

Putting LEDs into your models

LEDs (light emitting diodes) are brilliant for adding an extra twinkle to your model. They are low power, low-current drain (meaning that they last a long time on the same battery), and they can be very bright and small, so you can put them almost anywhere in a model or homemade toy. They are also very cheap.

> To add the finishing touches to an advanced model, nothing works better than a bit of light

A very quick and easy way to introduce an LED light to your model is to use the guts from a cheap key ring or penlight torch. You can use the torch exactly as is, just putting the whole thing in the model and arranging it so the button is easily accessible or pressed on by an extra bit of cardboard. As those little pen torches only cost a few cents, you can afford to put them in every model.

If you have some thin wire, separate the LED from the switch battery assembly so that you can mount the LED anywhere on the model and have the battery and switch unobtrusively somewhere else. Break open the key-ring-light housing and wrap one end of each of the thin wires round the LED legs and sticky-tape the other end of the wires to the battery/switch assembly. Take care that the polarity is the same as it was before, because the LED will not work and may be damaged if connected the wrong way across a battery.

On the web, you will find a massive range of very cheap LEDs for sale by mail order. Choose the hyperbright, flashing ones that have a built-in resistor, so that they can be wired straight to a 9 V battery without the need for any other components. You can use solder if you have a soldering iron, but wrapping wire tightly round the LED legs and sticking with tape is just as good for a model. A battery connector is useful for the battery end of the wires because the positive terminal of a PP3 9 V is very hard to wrap a wire around. If you have designed a toy or model so that the LED is only switched on while it is being played with, a 9 V PP3 battery will last the lifetime of the model and can be sealed up inside. This saves the complication of having to build a removable panel to change the battery.

happy making!

I have found the best way to give advice to your children is to find out what they want, and then advise them to do it.

HARRY S TRUMAN
33rd president of the United States

fluffy ladybug PAGE 35

space vase PAGE 20

fish doorhandles PAGE 43

space vase

Make a vase for real flowers—in minutes!

7 years +

20 minutes

Plastic bottles
Glue gun
Kitchen scissors
Craft knife

This is a fabulously simple project and a great one to get you going on the whole making-stuff thing. All you need are two old plastic bottles and you're on your way. For this one, we used a family-sized smoothie bottle for the base and a conditioner bottle for the flower holder. Given that these vases are so simple to make, why not put together a few and paint them in as many different ways as there are colors in the rainbow? The vase makes a great holder for the spooky flowers on page 24, and, as it holds water when finished, it's perfect for cut flowers, too.

1 Take two plastic bottles from hair care products or drinks, one long and slender, the other wide.

2 Keep the cap from the thin bottle, but cut its base off. To do this neatly, first mark a ring where you are going to cut, using a permanent marker.

3 Cut the shoulder portion from the wide bottle, removing the neck and all the body.

Glue the lid on to the thin bottle, invert it, and glue it into the open neck of the wide bottle. For the best effect, use a glue gun.

5 Paint, ideally using spray paint, although house emulsion might work if mixed with a single drop of dishwashing detergent.

Turn over the page to make some stunning flowers to display.

spooky flowers

Pompom blossoms from a plastic bag

12 years +

40 minutes

A4 paper sheet
Double-sided tape
White glue
Cardboard
Bin liner
Glue gun
Kitchen scissors
Paint

These flowers are wonderfully easy to make and you don't even need wool. The pompoms are made from plastic and can be any color you want, but for a really eerie feel, why not try black trash bags? The stems are made from a rolled-up piece of printer paper and and are a modern version of papier-mâché. The paper is rolled and glued using a coating of PVA glue to give a durable, woodlike stalk, and the stem is decorated with glue-gun glue to give long, delicate surface features. The whole lot is then painted black or silver (spray paint is best), with the raised features highlighted in a bright, contrasting color so that they glow against the dark paint. When you glue this stem into the black plastic pompom head, the end result is a beautiful table or window decoration.

The instructions here include a template sheet to trace over and help you make the pompom discs the perfect size.

spooky flowers

1 Stick a strip of double-sided tape diagonally across a sheet of A4 paper.

2 Roll the paper up very tightly diagonally so that you have a thin, rolled-up stem shape.

PVA GLUE

3 When you roll over the double-sided tape, stop and put a little PVA on the remaining paper.

4 (OPTIONAL) When the glue is dry, using the glue gun, make three stripes along the stem to give it an organic form.

5 Paint the stem black or silver with a paint that dries waterproof (spray or acrylic are ideal).

6 When the paint is dry, paint the glue-gun strips in a very bright dayglo color or even glow-in-the-dark paint.

X 2

7 Trace over the template provided and cut out two discs of thick cardboard.

spooky flowers

8 Cut a large black trash bag in half, top to bottom, and thread it through both discs, tightly wrapping it round and round.

11 Cut away the cardboard discs and trim to make a regular ball-shaped pompom.

9 When you can't wrap any more around it, slit the edge first with a craft knife and then with scissors.

12 Part the plastic folds and put some glue-gun glue at the center of the pompom.

10 Completely cut around the pompom until you can see the discs, then tightly tie a piece of string or plastic bag (if you want to be able to recycle it later) around the middle to secure.

13 Poke the stem up into the pompom. Support until set.

spooky flowers

pompom disc TEMPLATE **x 2**

chocolate rice krispie cakes

Delicious treats you don't even need to bake

7 years +	

15 mins to prepare,
20–30 mins to chill

Fork
Nonmetallic mixing bowl
Chip tube or drink bottle
Knife
Strong scissors
Mug

2 x 250 g Bar of chocolate
Stick of butter
1.5 x Mug dry Rice Krispies
1 tsp Sugar

This recipe is quick, easy, and great fun to make—nothing beats the sweet smell of melting chocolate. As well as guiding you through the recipe, we'll also show you how to form your own cupcake holders, so really this is a cooking and making project in one. The chocolate can be milk, white, or dark, just avoid using bars with flake chocolate or Mars as they contain ingredients that prevent them from melting properly. The exact quantity of ingredients isn't really important, but you will need enough chocolate to coat the Rice Krispies and enough of the cereal to fill some or all of your homemade cake rings. The recipe here should make twelve cakes, so enough for twelve kids or one very hungry kid!

chocolate rice krispie cakes

1 TEASPOON SUGAR

CHOCOLATE

1 The idea is that you don't need cupcake holders here; all you need is some little discs. So take either a chip tube or a small drink bottle and mark it off at roughly 15-mm intervals and then draw lines to the marks, making sure that they are neat.

2 Make the initial cut with a craft or kitchen knife and then cut out the rings with strong kitchen scissors.

3 You don't need baking paper—just lay a couple of sheets of plain paper on a suitable tray or flat surface and place the rings on that.

4 Break up one or two 250 g chocolate bars and place in a nonmetallic bowl with a small wedge of butter and a teaspoon of sugar (keeps the chocolate from setting too hard)

5 Microwave the chocolate, butter, and sugar mix on medium for about 10 seconds at a time, stirring between each burst, until the chocolate is melted and the butter and sugar are mixed in.

RICE KRISPIES

RICE KRISPIES

6 Gently stir the Rice Krispies into the melted mixture, trying not to crush too many.

▶

chocolate rice krispie cakes

7 Spoon the chocolate-covered Rice Krispies into the rings, then pat them down gently with the back of the spoon so that they are nice and flat.

8 Chill in the fridge for about 30 minutes, then press out.

TIP: While they are setting, why not make some wizard's sweet and cake boxes on page 190.

bottle-cap beetle

Lyra had one chasing her, AA Milne had one called Alexander, and Volkswagen made twenty-one million of them. Now you can make your own beetle from bottle caps in just a few minutes with this great little project designed by *Jellyfishguy*, a *dadcando* website member.

It's hard to believe how cool this beetle looks when you know that it is just three different-sized bottle caps. You need a tiny little toothpaste tube cap or flip lid for the head, a fizzy drink bottle lid or something similar for the body, and a larger, flatter lid like the one that comes off a one to four liter milk bottle for the carapace. Spray yours black like we have or make a fancy version with magical powers by spraying it gold and decorating it with runes.

To make your beetle, simply trace our leg and wing templates and follow these easy instructions.

A wicked-looking beetle made from junk

8 years +

30 minutes

Glue gun
  or fast resin glue
Black paint
Paper clips
Plastic bottle caps
Plastic food tray
Clear plastic
  packaging

bottle-cap beetle

1 Take one small plastic bottle cap from either a drink bottle or a household cleaner bottle, rest it on a piece of cardboard and draw around it with a permanent marker.

2 Cut out a smaller disc of cardboard to fit inside the bottle cap using the line you drew as a guide, and glue into the underside of the cap, flush with the bottom.

LEG TEMPLATE

3 Trace the template, then cut out six legs from a thin plastic food tray and glue three poking out from the bottom of the cap. Spray or paint the cap and a small toothpaste tube cap black.

WING TEMPLATE

4 Trace the template, then cut out four wing shapes from a piece of clear plastic packaging, draw two or three thin black lines on the wings, and then stick them on to the top of the cap as shown.

5 To make the head, glue the toothpaste tube lid onto the side of the bottle cap, opposite the wings.

6 To make the carapace, using strong scissors, cut a larger, flatter, soft bottle cap up one side and across most of the top. Use a milk bottle cap or something similar.

7 Using the scissors, cut a semicircle that is a little bit larger than the toothpaste tube cap out of the larger cap's side, then pull apart the two sides of the cap.

9 Stick the carapace to the body of the beetle so that it is up at an angle (use glue-gun glue) and hold the carapace in place until it is set. For the antennae, bend two paper clips and glue into the head.

8 Spray or paint the carapace.

Does your beetle need some company? Go to page 35 and make a ladybug to join him.

string nest

If glue and paper is called papier-mâché, then perhaps this method could be called *corde mâché,* with *corde* being the French word for string. String and white glue is a great craft combination. String is pliable and easy to drape around things when it is wet with PVA glue, but yet it dries hard and solid and is easy to paint. Building this nest makes a nice, satisfying mess, so you'll need to be wearing aprons or old clothes with your sleeves rolled up and have lots of newspaper to put down.

Use a nontoxic paint to paint the nest, and preferably one that dries waterproof—spray paint is ideal. Then fill the nest with bits of cotton wool and decorate the underside with leaves cut from green felt. If you are worried about the paint coming off on the eggs, simply fill your nest with little foil-wrapped ones. The end result makes a beautiful present.

string nest

1 Partially blow up a small balloon so that it is only about 10cm in diameter.

2 Rest the balloon in a jug or vase to support it.

WHITE GLUE

3 Cover the top of the balloon in white glue and lay some string pieces over the top. It helps to wet the string first in a mixture of water and white glue.

WHITE GLUE   WHITE GLUE

4 Cover with more white glue and start to wind string round the balloon, making sure that the string is covered with glue.

5 Wind more string around, adding glue as you do so that the string is wet, until you have covered about half of the balloon.

6 Allow to dry somewhere warm for 24 hours and then carefully remove the nest from the balloon.

▶

7 Paint or spray the nest dark brown (spray is certainly easier). If you want, you could add pieces of cotton wool or green felt leaves.

8 Fill the nest with little foil-wrapped eggs.

Visit our website to print gift tags you can color in.

fluffy ladybug

Getting this terrific spotted effect on a pompom is surprisingly easy when you know how, and you can choose any two colors you like to make this little bug. Ladybugs come in all shades of red, orange, and yellow, but why not have a go at making a bright blue or green one, too?

As with the spooky flowers earlier in this chapter, you can use plastic bags to make these pompoms, so there's nothing to stop you getting going right away. Black, white, or green trash bags work well, as do sandwich bags, which come in a range of subtle colors. As the ladybug's eyes are so small, when gluing them on, use a tiny spot of glue-gun glue on the head and put the eye on that. Be careful not to burn your fingers, and if you have a pin on hand, pick the eye up and position it with that.

Spotty wool —how will you do it?

7 years +

40 minutes

Wool (two colors)
Bottle cap
Paper clip
Cardboard
Detergent bottle
Bendy straws
Scissors
Glue gun
Beads

fluffy ladybug

1 Trace two disc template guides from the template on page 40. Glue the disc guides to a thin piece of cardboard and cut out two discs.

8 x 6.5 ft

2 Prepare the wool by doubling it up so that you have pieces about 6.5 ft long in bundles of about six to ten strands, depending on how thick the wool is. You may need three or four such bundles.

3 Starting with the body color, pass the wool through the hole in the middle of the disc repeatedly so that you wind it around the disc, until you have just covered it completely.

4 To make the spots, wind the spot color wool bundle only twice through in one place, and then, leaving a gap, do the same at another spot on the ring; space four or five of these bundle wrappings evenly around the disc.

5 When you have done this, cut off the remaining, contrasting color bundle and start a new bundle of the original body color. Wrap this around so that it covers up the spaced-out bundles completely. Carry on with this color until no more wool will pass through the middle of the disc.

6 Using strong scissors, push one blade of the scissors into the wool and between the two cardboard discs and cut the wool round the rim.

fluffy ladybug

7 Pass several short strands of the wool between the discs and tie tightly around the bundle and cut off below the ends of the pompom. DO NOT remove the cardboard discs, for now just put the tied-off pompom to one side while you make the body.

10 Trace the body template guides from the template page. Glue the guide to a thin piece of detergent bottle plastic and cut out carefully.

8 Spray or marker a small-drink bottle cap black. Use an office hole punch to cut some thin cardboard or detergent bottle plastic for the eyes, dot with a marker, and glue in place. Apply a spot of glue-gun glue to the bottle cap and position an eye on the end of a pin.

11 Spray or paint the body part black and stick the head in place.

x 6

9 Straighten two paper clips and poke through the cap top and glue inside the cap. Glue beads on the ends of the paper clips.

12 Cut six bendy drinking straws to about 4½ cm long so that the bendy bit is in the middle (use dark or black ones if you have them).

▶

fluffy ladybug

body TEMPLATE

GLUE

pompom disc TEMPLATE **x 2**

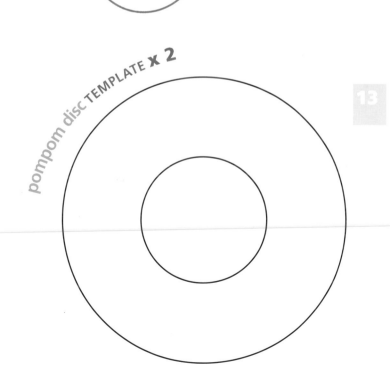

13 One by one, apply glue to the tabs on the body leg frame and push a straw on each tab, making sure that they are horizontal with the frame. When set, bend the straws to make the legs.

fluffy ladybug

14 Now take your pompom body and cut or push only one of the discs off the bundle and slide the body leg assembly into the pompom middle, over the remaining disc. When legs are in place, cut or push the other disc off the pompom.

15 Further bend the legs around so that your ladybird stands straight. Trim the pompom back very hard to get the right shape, especially underneath.

If a ladybug lands on you it's good luck, so make some luck for yourself with this fluffy pompom bug.

paper butterfly

A lovely little project that's just like a magic trick

8 years +

15 minutes

Wrapping paper
Strong thread

Make this beautiful butterfly in about five minutes using just a small scrap of old wrapping paper. This project is perfect if you are making your own greetings cards or simply want to decorate your room with something pretty.

When you've finished making the wings and have spread them out, you can customize your butterfly as much as you want. Make it out of brown paper and tie it off with parcel string to make a moth, or design a special butterfly all of your own by using plain paper and coloring it in with felt pens. You could also tie a small piece of pipe cleaner around the middle on the body to make the head, abdomen, and thorax of the butterfly, blob glue-gun glue on the body, and color it with marker, or stick beads or sequins to create beautifully iridescent butterfly scales.

paper butterfly

1 On any scrap piece of nice bright wrapping paper, draw a square about 3½ in x 3½ in, and a circle using the top of a glass or cup as a guide.

4 Continue to pleat the flap back and forth, making sure you keep it neat and in straight lines. This is not as easy as it looks, but it gets easier as you practice.

2 Carefully cut out the square and the circle and fold them both neatly in half.

5 Continue pleating until there is nothing more to fold, then turn the paper over and pleat up the other side. This is easier if you hold it in your hand rather than rest it on the table to fold it. Do the same with the circle.

3mm

3 Begin to pleat one side of the square with thin pleats. To pleat, fold the flap back on itself and then back the other way.

6 When both the square and circle are pleated, pinch them together between thumb and forefinger, tightly in the middle.

▶

7 Holding both pleated pieces together, tie some thread around their middle and tie it tightly in a knot. You'll need someone to help you do this.

9 . . . you can add a bit of pipe cleaner stuck on with white glue or glue-gun glue to make the butterfly's body.

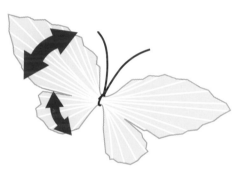

8 Fan out the square and the circle on both sides of the tie to make the four wings, and that's it. You can use the tie as the butterfly's antennae or...

Use a wire coathanger and some thread to create a beautiful butterfly mobile.

fish doorhandles

As Forrest Gump said, "It's funny what a young man recollects." Like him, I don't remember being born, nor what I got for my first birthday, but I do remember the pattern on the curtains in my first bedroom—African animals running across an ochre linen landscape as the fabric fluttered in the gentle breeze.

It's the unique little details on handmade things that make them into something that we become attached to, and that help turn our houses into homes. Bright colors, stencil painting, or funky handles can transform even the most boring piece of furniture into a flight of fancy.

These simple fish handles make an exciting, mesmerizing, and memorable accessory and will bring any kid's room to life.

Brighten up a bedroom and inspire your kids

12 years +
3 hours

Jigsaw
Drill
Small piece of wood
  or MDF sheet
Threaded screw with
  nut
Small section of
  metal tubing
Newspaper
Wood glue
Glue gun
Paint

fish doorhandles

1 Trace the template and stick it to a small piece of thin plywood or MDF sheet about 1 cm thick, and carefully cut out both fish shapes using a jigsaw. For simplicity, the instructions only show the big fish being made, however, follow each step for the small fish as well.

2 Drill a stepped hole in the center of each fish. Drill the large hole first (only halfway through the wood), then drill the small hole. Be careful not to drill into the table or bench you are resting the work on. It's best to use an old bit of wood underneath to support your work piece and protect your table.

3 Push a long, thin, threaded bolt (about 6 cm, M4) through the hole so that the bolt head is flush with the top of the wood. Fill over the bolt head with glue so that the bolt is firmly fixed in place.

4 Carve, file, or sandpaper the edges of the wooden shape to soften the top of the fish. To save time building up the shape, stick a slightly smaller cardboard-fish shape to the top face of the fish. For the best effect, the tongue and the fins should be thinner than the body.

5 Add additional details using repeated applications of glue-gun glue. This will speed up the project and reduce the number of papier-mâché layers needed to get a nicely shaped fish. The fish does not need to be shaped on the back.

fish doorhandles

6 Cover the fish in papier-mâché strips. Use thin strips of newspaper dipped in watered-down, white woodwork glue (PVA). Water down using two parts glue to one part water. Cover the entire fish, smoothing out or building up features as desired.

little fish **TEMPLATE**

big fish **TEMPLATE**

fish doorhandles

7 Allow the fish to dry out completely before painting. While it is drying, cut two short lengths of tubing to use as spacers for the bolt fixings, so that the handles will stand proud on the door. Metal curtain rod is ideal, but any narrow tube will do; you could even use a felt pen or ballpoint pen barrel.

8 When the papier-mâché is completely dry, usually overnight or at least after a few hours in a drying rack, paint it white with water-based house emulsion. Then, when that is dry, put a blob on glue round the base of the bolt and glue the spacer tube into place.

9 Paint and varnish your fish. Choose bright exciting colors—look on the web for pictures of tropical fish, or even make up some fantastic designs of your own. Finally drill a small hole in your cupboard door and fit the new handles. Use a small washer under the nut if necessary to stop the nut pulling through the door wood.

TIP: The handles overlap slightly, so arrange them so that the little one doesn't extend on to the opposite door and close that one first.

BIG-KITCHEN SCIENCE
Felt-pen chromatography

Experiments in the kitchen are really good fun. This one shows which dyes are used to make the colors in children's felt pens, and as well as being quick and enjoyable, it's also highly scientific. The experiment can be used as a basis for some interesting discussions about color and the fact that even dye molecules have different

weights (*mass,* if you want to get technical). It will reinforce things your kids will be learning at school at some point, and the resulting strips can be dried out and kept in the special booklet that you can print out from our website.

Keep any discussion about the experiment brief and to the point so that they don't lose interest. On page 51, you'll find an experimental discussion outline with a few key interesting facts. This is designed to help you fire up your children's interest, and to simply explain what's going on in the experiment if they ask.

Find out what dyes are used in your felt pens

I don't believe in dumbing things down for children; they are learning machines hungry for interesting bits of information. As long as you use words that they understand, you'll find that kids of any age readily grasp new concepts. Discuss the experiment with them as you are doing it. At the same time, make sure you listen to what they are saying, because when they are relaxed and having fun, the things they talk about are a good window on how they are thinking and feeling.

6 years +

20 minutes

Blotting paper or
   coffee filter paper
Scissors
Wire coathanger
Plastic packaging

download available

1 Cut some strips of blotting paper or white coffee filter paper about 1 cm x 15 cm. Fold about 15 mm.

2 Cut the long piece from a wire coathanger and bend into a stand like this.

3 Mark, then trim the bottom off a plastic packaging container (e.g., cream cheese package) to make the water reservoir about 1½ cm high.

4 Hang strip on stand and trim so that it is able to hang freely with the bottom edge about 2–3 mm from the bottom of the reservoir.

USE A WATER-BASED FELT-TIP

5 Fill the reservoir with water to a depth of about ½ cm.

6 Draw a single, short horizontal line of the desired color 10 mm from the bottom of the blotting paper strip.

7 Color a small square of the same color on a piece of normal paper, cut out, and stick to the strip about two-thirds of the way up.

8 Hang the strip on the stand so its end dips in the water, making sure the felt pen line is above the water level.

9 When colors are separated out, remove strip and lay on another piece of blotting paper to dry.

Experimental discussion

What makes the water go up the blotting paper?

The attraction of the water to the blotting paper molecules is stronger than the forces holding the water molecules to each other (this is called *capillary action*).

Why does the ink separate out?

The different dyes used to make up the felt-tip colors are made of molecules of different weights and the water can carry the less heavy dye molecules further up.

What are the primary colors?

Red, blue, and yellow. These are colors that can't be mixed using other colors. Any two of the primary colors mixed together makes a secondary color. These are the reflective primary colors. The primary colors of light (transmissive colors) are red, green, and blue (RGB).

How is chromatography used in the real world?

Scientists use a range of solvents (like the water that you used) to find out which molecules are in chemicals. DNA is separated out using a similar process of molecular dye markers in a gel.

When it really matters

We are children for only 20 percent of our lives. It's a busy time, too. We learn how to speak, we become self-aware, we understand what it is to be loved and unloved. At different times we experience neglect, varying degrees of physical and emotional threats (such as bullying or punishment), and we learn how to live as an individual. Our parents are not only our protectors and caregivers but also our most important role models. How we see them having fun, dealing with difficult situations, working through the fallout from arguments, solving problems, or just generally coping with life, starts a tape running in our head that plays back over and over throughout the rest of our lives. These experiences shape our own behaviors and personal relationships.

Children are the most incredible learning machines, actively following and learning from the nuances of what we, their parents, do rather than what we say. Even with the best will in the world, no one can get it right all the time. So when you go wrong, just mentally go back to this list and try harder next time to help your kids to grow into happy, successful, confident people.

1 Be reliable

Make every effort to do what you say you're going to do and don't make promises you can't keep. If you agree to pick them up from school or go to a school event, write the date down or set an alarm on your phone as a reminder. It's very easy to forget the exact details and end up letting your kids down.

2 Be a grown-up

In any conflict or difficult interaction with your children, remember that you are the adult. Don't start arguing with your children at their level. If they are doing something wrong, you need to tell them what it is and show and tell them how you expect them to behave. Stay in control of your emotions and you will stay in control of the situation. Never threaten a punishment you can't or don't expect to deliver.

3 Build and keep to a routine

Setting up and keeping to a routine is what dads are good at. Moving to a new neighborhood, homes going to a new school, or the arrival of a new baby are stressful periods of change that are very unsettling for children, so even doing a simple activity at the same time, every day or week, will become something they can rely on. This could be something as straightforward as getting ice cream on Saturday afternoons or always having their favorite meal on a certain night.

4 Listen to your kids

The little things your children say and do will give you a good idea about how they are feeling. Changes in the way your children do and say things could indicate they are experiencing feelings of anxiety. Try to think outside of the immediate problem and look at the bigger picture. Most importantly, listen. It's all too easy to forget to listen to your children when you are preoccupied with your own problems of a stressful day at work or bills that need to be paid.

5 Work together as Parents

Moms and dads argue; even the best parents in the world disagree. However, never make nasty, snide, or cynical comments about your children's mother to them. They love their mother unconditionally because she is their mother, just as they love you unconditionally because you are their father. However much you may feel

BEING THERE

wronged by your partner after an argument, your children don't need to know. Never argue about your children's discipline in front of your children. Work together as parents to present a united front and work through your differences later when the children aren't around.

6 Add excitement to their lives

As the big kid of the family, you're the best person for the job. Excitement can be brought into children's lives in many ways, and not just by endless presents. Think of the smaller ways to add fun to their lives. This could be with something as simple as putting a weird candy sprinkles topping on a pancake you just made together or putting a plastic fish into the clear-liquid soap dispenser in the bathroom.

7 Support your kids

To understand your children better, engage with them on a personal level. If you don't already know their best friends' names or who their favorite (and least favorite) teacher is, then make an effort to find out. Don't make it an inquisition—everyone needs their privacy—just pay attention when they volunteer the information. Taking the time to pay attention to the details of what is important in their lives when they are young will show that you are interested in the things outside your relationship that mean something to them. This will have huge benefits as they grow up and they continue to trust you with information about what they are getting into as teenagers, when losing touch with them as people is a real possibility.

8 Take them to school

If possible, organize your work week so that you can take your children to, or pick them up from, their school one day each week. It might be difficult, but the benefits are worth it. School is a major part of your children's lives and their routine, and understanding just a little bit of it will help you connect with them. If it's not possible for you to do a school run, then make the time once during each year to spend one whole day helping out at their school. Schools are always looking for parent involvement and have special event days that require extra help, so you'll find a warm welcome if you contact the school and ask them what you can do.

9 Read to them at bedtime

Bedtime is an important routine for your children and making story telling part of it will make it a time that everyone looks forward to. Aim to do it every night, but if you can't do it every weeknight because of work commitments, then make it a weekend routine. As they get older, choose stories that you know will stretch their imagination and stories that you will enjoy reading. Act out different voices for the characters; they won't notice if the voices are all wrong, but they'll love the fun of it, and it will let them relax and enjoy the time together, knowing that you are having fun and enjoying it, too.

10 Spend time with your children

Made With Dad is about spending quality time with your children. It's simple—that is what they need. Spending quality time with you will ensure that they grow up into happy, balanced individuals. Toys and treats are no substitute for quality time. In your busy life, time is a valuable commodity. Your children, who crave your attention, know the value of your time, and will benefit from every minute you give them.

space rocket PAGE 162

You know—fathers just have a way of putting everything together.

Anonymous

doughnut PAGE 57

kokeshi doll PAGE 73

big-kitchen science
MOLECULAR-BUILDING KIT 84

being there
BE PREPARED 87

jean pencil case PAGE 54

jean pencil case

Encourage the artist in your kids by making this really useful pencil case together

	12 years +
	1 hour

Rectangle of fabric
Glue gun
Pencil

If you've got an old pair of jeans that you no longer wear, don't throw them away—make them into something. A pencil roll is a must for any budding artist, and is just what you need to keep all your best sketching pencils neatly in order and in perfect condition.

We've made our pencil roll from old denim (there's something so cool about that) but of course, any old trousers, curtains, canvas, upholstery, or other reasonably robust fabric will work just as well. We've used a glue gun to make the whole thing, which means you don't need a sewing machine. However, if you have a sewing machine, just replace the glue gun instruction steps with sewing machine ones, and you'll get an excellent result.

jean pencil roll

1 Cut a square of fabric from the leg of some old jeans; use the full circumference of the leg and a height of about 14 in. You can use any thick canvas like fabric.

For this project, we will be using a glue gun for all the seams, but you can just as easily use a sewing machine if you have one or other fabric glue.

2 Fold over a small edge seam around each edge of about ½–1 cm and glue in place all around.

3 Using either a pencil or ballpoint pen, on the inside of the material, mark some guidelines as shown. Start by drawing the horizontal lines at 3½ in and then 3 in and 1½ in, then draw the vertical lines about 1 in apart.

4 Put thin, neat vertical strips of glue between the bottom two horizontal lines over the vertical lines you have marked. Work quickly to avoid the glue setting and only glue half the lines before carefully folding over the bottom flap to cover them.

5 When the first bit of glue has set, gently peel back the free, unglued part and continue applying glue to the other vertical marks before folding the bottom flap up again and gluing completely in place.

▶

jean pencil roll

6 Put a thin strip of glue down each corner edge and glue the bottom edges neatly together and then fold over the smaller top flap and glue along the edge at each end.

7 Use a glue gun to glue a small rectangle of hook and eye fastener at the extreme edge of the top and bottom flaps (as shown).

8 To make sure that the other part of the hook and eye fastener is in the right place, loosely roll up the pencil case (or roll up tightly with pencils inside) and mark where the other part of the fastener should go. Then glue in exactly the right place.

Displays your pencils in a really handy way and also protects them from getting broken.

doughnut

Make this delicious-looking treat, just like the doughnuts Homer Simpson loves so much, in under an hour. All you'll need are two lightweight grocery bags, some sticky tape, and a bit of glue-gun glue. Prepare to step into the world of modern, no-wait papier-mâché!

This is papier-mâché with a difference. Instead of bits of paper, you are going to use old grocery bags to give your model bulk and form, and instead of wet glue, you are going to use masking tape, so you won't have to wait for ages for it to dry. This is really a very easy model to make, and it will show you how you can use glue-gun glue to do a form of rudimentary modeling. Be careful when using the glue gun and read the section on page 16 for tips on safe use.

A plastic-bag doughnut that looks good enough to eat!

| 12 years + |
| 1 hour |

Masking tape
Glue gun
Spray paint
Sprinkles

doughnut

1 Curl one lightweight, plastic grocery bag around into a doughnut shape and wrap in masking (or normal sticky) tape.

2 Take a second bag, tear in half lengthways, and wrap around the doughnut until it looks about the right thickness.

3 Wrap the doughnut in masking tape so that it is as smooth as possible.

4 Coat the top of the doughnut in a liberal layer of glue-gun glue so that some dribbles down the side.

5 Do one half at a time, but coat the second half while the first is still hot so that the edges merge. Don't put too much on, otherwise it will run everywhere. **Note: glue-gun glue is hot and will burn if it gets on you.**

6 (Ideally) spray the top of the doughnut with bright pink paint. It doesn't matter if you get overspray on the rest of the doughnut, because you will be painting over that later. Make it a nice thick layer. Then while the spray paint is still wet...

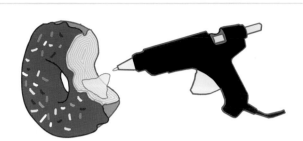

7 Sprinkle rainbow sprinkles over the top of the doughnut so that they stick in the wet paint. If you don't have spray paint, then you can get this effect by painting white glue (PVA, that dries clear) over your pink paint and sprinkling the sugar strands on to that while it is wet.

10 To make the filling, build up a big blob of glue-gun glue.

8 Cut through glue-gun glue with a strong craft knife and then cut the tape and plastic bag doughnut with a pair of scissors or long thin knife in a sawing action. If you don't want a bite then skip to step 14.

11 The blob will want to sag or drip, so keep turning doughnut as it sets (see next two steps).

9 Seal the cut face with a thin layer of glue-gun glue.

12 Build up the blob over two or three tries; a big blob of hot glue takes much longer to set and will be hard to control.

▶

doughnut

13 There are two blobs of filling; do one side at a time, adding more glue and letting it set until it looks right.

15 Paint the bread part of the bite a lighter shade of brown than the outside of the doughnut and then paint the blueberry filling a nice rich purple.

14 Paint the sides of the doughnut with acrylic paint. Paint the sides slightly darker than the bottom. Mix up a light brown (use more yellow and white in the mix) or use yellow ochre if you have it.

Looks great on a plate, but why not put your doughnut in a box frame and turn your pop tart into pop art!

bookbinding

Now you can bind your own hardback book in the same way that bookbinders have been doing it for generations. All you need are some spare sheets of paper, old cardboard, and almost any leftover pieces of fabric or leather. Make a holiday book, personalized diary, or a special birthday book, and to add a personal touch, simply print out a header and footer on the pages before you bind them. This project shows you the basics, but after you have made your first book, you might want to experiment with binding in different types of paper.

For the cover, you can use almost any material: specially bought fabric, leather from an old coat or handbag, felt, curtains, old cushion covers. Josie, a *dadcando* website member, customized her denim book cover by gluing one of the jeans pockets on to the front of the book to keep her pens and pencils in.

A beautiful sheet of marbled lining paper is available to print out from our website.

A beautiful hardback book made and bound by you

12 years +
1 hour (incl. glue drying)
Paper PVA glue Cardboard Fabric Stapler Colored paper or marbled printable
download available

bookbinding

 Take eight A4 sheets of paper and stack them neatly.

Fold the whole stack over as neatly as possible.

Unfold the stack. Turn the stack over and make sure that all the pages are still aligned.

If you don't have a long arm stapler, open up a normal office stapler.

Using a slow, firm action, press a staple out through the paper and into an eraser positioned under the paper.

Staple both ends about 2cm in from the edge and turn over, then carefully fold over the open staples with your thumb or a suitable blunt edge. Ideally make four (or more) of these eight-sheet pages.

bookbinding

7 Cut a piece of thin fabric (ideally cotton or something similar) in a strip as long as the pages and five times the width of them together.

8 Holding the pages tightly together, glue the edges of the spines with glue-gun glue or PVA glue (only covering the edges).

9 Press the pages' spine onto the fabric, taking care not to glue the fabric to the sides by mistake.

10 If you want, you can now trim the pages so that they have a neat edge. This takes practice. Be very careful with the craft knife.

11 Place the pages on some old stiff cardboard and draw around it, allowing a border of about ½ cm.

12 Cut out two of the same-sized book covers (cut one then trace around it for the second).

13 Assemble the covers and the pages, and using a piece of scrap cardboard, measure the depth of the combined covers and pages together.

bookbinding

14 Using the depth marker, cut a strip of cardboard for the spine, the same height as the cover pieces.

15 Lay out the covers and spine on a piece of fabric or leather so that they are all aligned and are spaced two thicknesses of cardboard apart. Then mark the fabric with a border of about 1 in all around and neatly cut out to the mark.

16 Glue the covers and spine in place using PVA (white glue) or Copydex. Spread evenly, using a scrap of cardboard as a spatula.

17 Glue the border over as neatly as possible, taking care with the corners. For thicker fabrics, you might have to cut off some of the hidden corner fold to avoid it being too bulky at the corners.

18 Apply glue to, and spread evenly over, only the center-most parts of the cover (NOT THE SPINE).

19 Glue the flaps from the spine-binding fabric to the covers (DO NOT GLUE IT TO THE COVER SPINE).

22 Fold over your lining paper and glue one-half at a time to the front page and to the inside of the front cover. Repeat for the back.

20 Print out the downloadable marbled paper, make your own, or buy some and cut out.

21 Neatly paste the first page and the inside of the cover with glue. Make the glue even and paste right up to the edge.

Why not bind in different types of paper, tissue, or tracing paper, or perhaps dark, rich-colored, or black paper, to make a lovely, old-fashioned photograph album or scrapbook?

painted egg

Learn the ancient art of egg blowing and then paint beautiful eggs like these

8 years +

45 minutes
(incl. glue drying)

1 Hen's egg
Glue gun
Cocktail stick
Scissors
Paint (that dries
waterproof)

download available

There is something about the fragility of an egg, coupled with its small size and simplicity, which has always fascinated artists. Then there's the whole art of blowing an egg; an exciting experiment all of its own. However, once you start painting the blown egg, you quickly realize that the hardest part is actually holding the thing steady while painting it. This project shows you how to make a special little holder to make sure that you can easily paint your egg for the best results.

Using good, fluid, bright paints and a nice, new, thin brush will make the job much more satisfying. If you design your egg first, you can go out together to the craft or art shop and buy a few little tins of quick-drying enamel and a small brush as part of the activity.

painted egg

1 Gently wash the egg in cold, soapy water, and then rinse and dry.

2 Carefully using the tip of a sharp craft knife, rotate back and forth on the same spot until you make a small hole at one end.

3 It can take up to five minutes to make a neat hole. Don't rush or force the blade, because then you will crack the egg. Do the same at both ends. Run a cocktail stick through the egg to pierce the inner membrane.

4 Gently hold the egg to your lips and blow the contents out. Rinse the inside of the egg under a tap and by blowing water through it.

5 Put some glue-gun glue on the end of a cocktail stick and glue the stick into the egg at one end. Hold steady till it is set.

6 Trace the egg holder template onto a piece of thick cardboard and carefully cut it out using scissors or a craft knife.

7 Fold up the egg holder and stick the corners using glue-gun glue or sticky tape.

painted egg

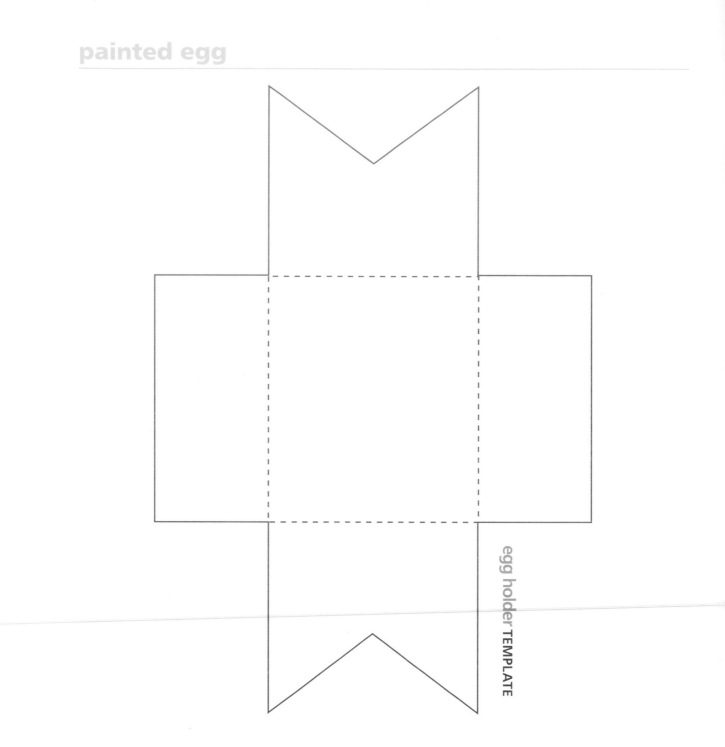

egg holder TEMPLATE

8   Design your egg pattern or visit our website to print out some design templates.

9   Spray or paint the egg a bright color to start with; it gives you a head start and makes the egg look nice right away.

10   Place the egg in the holder and paint your design. Rotate the egg using the tips of the cocktail stick, resting your hand on a book pushed up to the holder.

11   When your egg is dry, very carefully work the cocktail stick loose or cut it off with a pair of strong scissors.

Display your egg in a nest, or turn the page to make your own egg stand.

egg stand

What better way to display your handblown, painted eggs than with this delicate egg stand?

You can use thick paper or medium-weight cardboard to make this great-looking egg stand. Print out a colored stand in ebony or cherry from our website or make your own in ivory, jade, silver, or gold, using the outline templates provided. This is a really simple, good-looking project that will give you the perfect platform to show off your handpainted pieces.

12 years +

1 hour
(incl. glue drying)

Paper
PVA glue
Cardboard
Fabric
Stapler
Colored paper or
marbled printable

download available

egg stand

TAB CORNER

1 Trace the egg stand template on page 74 onto a medium-weight cardboard or thick, stiff paper if you have it. If not, trace onto normal paper and stick it to a piece of thin cardboard.

Carefully cut out using a craft knife or strong scissors.

2 Alternatively, use either the cherry or ebony printables, or use the blank outlines and color your own stand to look like jade (green), ivory (very pale yellow), gold, or silver. Carefully cut out using a craft knife or strong scissors.

3 Turn over the cutout and make a deep crease from corner to corner on the back on the three corners that have folds; that is, the two main corners and the one with the tab.

GLUE

4 Turn back over and fold the stand at the creases.

Put a blob of glue-gun glue or PVA on the tab (this will take a while to dry and will need to be held while drying) or stick a small piece of double-sided sticky tape onto the tab.

▶

egg stand

egg stand 1 TEMPLATE

egg stand 1 TEMPLATE

egg stand 2 TEMPLATE

5 Glue the tab neatly to the inside of the free corner. Color the cut cardboard edges in with a similar colored marker.

Now your stand is ready to present your painted eggs.

Make a Victorian glass dome and show off your painted egg and stand to perfection (see p. 234).

kokeshi doll

Kokeshi (小芥子), are simple Japanese dolls made from wood that came from Northern Japan in the seventeenth century. The beauty of this project is that you can make one in a few minutes or spend the whole afternoon on design, spraying, and careful painting— the only limit is your imagination.

All you need for the head and hair are two old packaging lids of slightly different sizes. For the head, the lid needs to have a rounded top, which you will turn upside-down to make the curved, visible bit of the face, with the bigger lid forming the hair. For the body, you can use a simple product bottle cut down to size.

So try your hand at making a Kokeshi doll. Approach it with peace and create your very own lucky charm.

One of the most collectible toys in Japan— now you can make your own!

| 8 years + |
| 30 minutes |

Spray or roll-on deodorant caps
Bottles
Glue gun

kokeshi doll

1 Look for a small plastic bottle with simple curves. Hair products and mini yogurt drinks are suitable. Also, you will need two large aerosol or roll-on deodorant caps of slightly different sizes so that one fits over the other.

always mark before cutting

2 Search on the web for pictures of Kokeshi dolls that you would like to copy. Mark on the bottle and the product pack lids and cut out using strong scissors. The fringe should be low so that only a small bit of face is showing.

3 If you have very fine wet and dry emery paper (p600 or finer), rub down the plastic bottle to provide a key for the paint, then paint or spray the bottle a nice bright color. If you have more than one color, blend between them.

4 Take the larger of the two caps and after rubbing down the surface with fine emery paper, spray or paint it a suitable dark color. You can hold the piece on a slightly crushed, cardboard toilet paper tube, pushed inside the cap.

5 Decorate the body of the doll using paints and permanent felt-tip pen markers. Look at traditional Kokeshi dolls on the web and try to learn about how the Kokeshi doll maker stylishly portrays a simple face, then copy it.

6 Glue the head to the top of the bottle and the hair over the head. Kokeshi dolls are simple and elegant. Practice this simple project until you are able to convey some of those unique and peaceful qualities in your dolls.

Check on the web for Kokeshi doll designs to inspire you and think up more along the lines of ninjas, manga, or sumo.

paint a shirt

Painting a T-shirt is really easy; it's the perfect way to spend the afternoon, and your kid will have something great to wear at the end of it. Fabric paint is not expensive, and if you buy just a few colors, you can mix a bit of acrylic paint with them to get the exact color you want.

The key with any designing or making project is to have a good idea of what you want to do before you actually start making it. All you have to do is start with something you like. Simplify it in your mind or on paper, so that you are not making your job too difficult—remember: simpler is better. More often the images that look best on a T-shirt are the simple, striking ones, so get sketching right away. Any extra effort you put in at the beginning getting the design right will pay off in the finished article.

All you need to know to make a fun and original T-shirt

| 7 years + |
| 90 minutes |
| Plain white T-shirt
Fabric paint
Paintbrush and
    marker
Clothes iron |

paint a shirt

1 The most important part of any good project is the design. Start by designing your T-shirt on a sheet with some T-shirt shapes drawn on it. Use references from a book, a DVD, or your favorite video game.

2 Once you have a design that you are happy with, enlarge it onto a separate piece of paper. You can enlarge it by eye or by photocopier. Use a thick black marker to draw the outline. Don't color the picture in at this stage because you need it to be as clear as possible so that you can see it through the T-shirt fabric.

3 Next you will need to slightly stretch your T-shirt to provide a good surface to paint on. Put some flat cardboard or an up-turned tea tray inside the T-shirt. To make sure that it doesn't move while you are painting, stick the shirt to the board with a few small pieces of sticky tape.

4 Slip the enlarged design under the fabric, on top of the board, and position it exactly where you want it to be. Now carefully begin to paint the T-shirt, following the design that you can just see through the fabric. You will need a smallish brush with only a little bit of paint on it at a time. Be careful not to overload your brush, as the paint will bleed into the T-shirt fabric and make blobs on your design. Be very careful not to smudge your hand across the parts that you have already painted. Start with the light colors and paint the darker ones over the top of them. IMPORTANT: Fabric paint does not wash out of clothes, so make sure you are wearing old painting clothes or an apron—BEFORE you start!

5 Once you have finished painting your design, leave the T-shirt to dry for about 15 minutes. Then carefully remove the stretching board and the template image. Be careful not to drag them out because they might still have wet paint on them, and this will mark the inside of the shirt, which could show through. Dry the shirt using a hairdryer if you have one. You want the shirt to be finished quickly, otherwise, leave it to dry for an hour or so in a warm place.

6 When the design is completely dry, turn the T-shirt inside out and place an old hand towel inside it. This is a precaution in case the paint isn't completely dry (which invariably it isn't). Then iron over the design with the iron on its hottest setting (fabric permitting) to fix the design. The hottest setting is fine for most natural fabrics (like cotton), but if you have used a manmade material, check the label to see what the maximum setting of the iron can be before starting. ALWAYS supervise children if they are using an iron. Turn right side out and wear your T-shirt with pride at every opportunity.

For a simpler option, inkjet out a web image or photo from your digital camera and use iron-on, transfer-printing paper to make a permanent design.

micro cans

Make these cute mini tin cans for action figures and dolls

| 8 years + |
| 15 minutes |
| Glue gun |
| Hacksaw |
| Craft knife |
| Old felt-pen lids |
| Tin foil |
| download available |

This is a really simple model, quick to make, and there are so many possibilities. These tiny micro cans are absolutely perfect for action figures, where the tins can be made into army rations, or for small dolls. You can use the label printouts provided on our website to get you started, but it's far better if you and your kids design labels of your own. To do this, you'll need to draw the labels bigger, with normal felt pens and pencils, scan them into your computer, reduce them to the right size, and then print them out. Alternatively, you could reduce them in size on a photocopier.

It really is as easy as it looks; the instructions show you how to make sure that they are all the same size. This project should take you about 10 minutes per can, less if you really get good at making them.

micro cans

1 Take any old felt-pen lid, the best ones for the templates are 10 mm to 11 mm in diameter. The color doesn't matter as it will all be covered up with straight sides.

4 Put a blob of glue-gun glue in one end of the sawn-off lid, being careful not to get any on the outside of the lid.

2 Carefully cut out a piece of paper 1 in x 5 in and stick around the lid using sticky tape.

3 Using the edge of the paper as a guide, saw the lid crosswise with a metal hacksaw (this is a great safe way for kids to practice sawing).

5 Turn over the lid and press it down hard onto a small scrap of tin foil resting on a sponge, so that it dents in.

6 When the foiled end has cooled slightly, put a blob of glue-gun glue in the open end, turn over, and repeat with another scrap of foil.

7 Trim the waste foil away so that the end and some of the sides are covered.

8 Carefully cut out one of the label templates, or make your own label, and wrap around the end of the lid so that the same amount of lid sticks out of each end. Stick with double-sided tape or use clear sticky tape.

Get creative and make spilled cans or open cans with their lids still attached.

micro books

Long car journeys from here to there are special weekends away; kids these days often have to do a lot of traveling and have a lot to keep in their heads. So, what better than a pocket-sized notebook to write and sketch down all those important thoughts? These fun little origami micro books are a really simple project that anyone can tackle. They're perfect for kids as they're small enough to fit in a pocket or a small bag and they don't have loads of pages that will never get written on. My kids showed me how to make a micro book in about five minutes; it's that quick and easy. See our website for graphic printables including holiday diaries that are perfect for keeping happy memories of a lovely time with Dad.

Catch all those important thoughts in this neat little notebook

7 years +
5 minutes
Sheet of A4 paper
download available

micro books

1. Place paper printed side down on a flat surface.

2. Fold in half lengthwise, making sure that you fold carefully to make a straight, neat fold.

3. Unfold.

4. Now fold in half crossways, again making sure that you fold carefully to make a straight fold.

5. Fold in half crossways again. This is a bit harder because you are folding two thicknesses of paper, but still make sure you are accurate.

6. Now unfold the last fold you just made.

7. Carefully cut along the middle fold only halfway across the folded paper as shown.

8. Now, unfold the piece of paper completely so that it is A4 size again.

9. Still with printed side down, fold in half lengthwise.

10. Rotate the whole piece so that it can stand on the table or so that you can hold it upright.

micro books

11 Gripping both ends between the thumbs and forefingers of both hands, push ends together.

12 Push ends together until you make a cross shape as shown, then fold the pages around to one side to make your book, making sure the front one is on the outside.

GLUE   GLUE

13 If you want to make a really neat job of it, you can add a small dab of glue just inside both of the open corners (a glue stick is fine for this purpose).

14 Rub the spine carefully with the back of a fingernail to make sure the booklet keeps its shape and stays closed.

Use a blank micro book to write and illustrate your first mini novel.

Molecular-building kit

Turn your kitchen into a molecular factory

This is a great little project and you can make some really cool molecules if you have a few minutes and a handful of bits and pieces. The molecule shown here is methane (CH_4). This is the molecule that scientists look for when searching for extraterrestrial life. More about that in a minute, but first let's talk about atoms.

8 years +
2 hours

Deodorant balls
Cocktail sticks
Drinking straws

Atoms are the building blocks of all matter, and when they are found on their own, they are called *elements*. An atom is made up of a positively charged *nucleus* (itself made of *protons*) surrounded by negatively charged particles called *electrons*.

Carbon dioxide is made up of one carbon atom joined to two oxygen atoms. Plants respire using carbon dioxide, and use it in the presence of sunlight to make energy in a process called *photosynthesis*. The by-product is oxygen, useful for us and all the other animals on earth that need oxygen to live. *Methane* is a smelly gas made up of one carbon atom and four hydrogen atoms.

Water is the most common molecular compound on earth and is fundamental to life. Freezing at 32°F and boiling at 212°F, it covers almost 70 percent of the earth's surface. It is nature's most powerful solvent, dissolving most things to some degree. It's strange to think of that clear liquid being made up of two highly reactive, invisible gases, but it is—water consists of one oxygen joined to two hydrogen atoms. To build your molecular models, you will need some roll-on deodorant balls. You won't need many because you can reuse them in loads of different arrangements.

1 Deodorant roll-on balls are great for molecule making.

2 To remove the ball safely, poke the tip of a pair of small scissors between the pack and the ball and cut three or four slits in the soft-pack plastic and pop the roller ball out.

3 Either wait and collect the deodorant balls, or just buy the cheapest deodorant and pour the deodorant away, or save in another container to refill other packs later.

4 Mark the balls with small dots where you are going to drill. Look on the web to find what different molecules look like and how their bonds are traditionally shown. Start simple.

5 Drill a very small hole through the ball surface. Use a drill that is a tight fit for a cocktail stick or piece of wire coathanger.

6 Holding the ball on a spare piece of cocktail stick or coathanger wire, spray or paint a nice bright color.

7 Cut some equal-sized lengths of drinking straw (or any lightweight tubing) using a pair of scissors.

30mm

8 Push stick into hole and thread piece of straw followed by another ball. Use glue if you want a permanent structure.

9 If the black ball is a carbon atom and the pink ones are hydrogen atoms, then this is methane—smelly!

Experimental discussion

Who is credited with coming up with the stick and ball molecular model?

Niels Bohr, a Danish scientist (1885–1962).

How big is an atom?

Very small, about one ten-millionth of a millimeter in diameter.

What is an element?

An *element* is the most basic type of matter that is composed of only one type of atom. Hydrogen (H), oxygen (O), carbon (C), and iron (Fe) are examples of elements.

What is a molecule?

A *molecule* is a compound made up when two or more atoms join together. Water (H_2O), carbon dioxide (CO_2), methane (CH_4), and common salt (sodium chloride, NaCl) are typical molecular compounds.

BEING THERE

Be prepared

The moments you have with your children are precious. If you're busy all week, that can put a lot of pressure on the weekends and that valuable quality time. As a result, the weekend can end up being stressful, and overexcitement can lead to arguments, headaches, and other minor upsets, which are physical ways of expressing the emotional stresses and strains of breaking a routine or things not quite panning out like they were meant to. If you are prepared for any situation, you can get a few extra hero points by being able to save the day and get your weekend (or special evening) back on track quickly and easily.

When things start to go wrong that threaten to spoil your special time, take a deep breath and don't panic. If it's just a minor upset, then don't let it get to you. Remember, you are in this for the long game, and there'll always be next weekend.

Some of these tips might seem a bit simple, but for me they have been the most useful things that I have done to be prepared.

1 Keep some simple emergency medicines in your home

Be prepared to manage minor illnesses. There is nothing worse than a child getting sick at night when you can't go out or when the pharmacy is closed. Pick these items up the next time you are at the supermarket. There's no need to buy brand name medicine; supermarket brands are much cheaper and just as good. To be prepared for the most common, rapid-onset, minor children's complaints, such as mild headaches, toothaches, stomach aches, cuts and bruises, or slight fevers, you will need:

- 1 bottle children's acetaminophen syrup
- 1 bottle children's ibuprofen syrup
- 1 bottle milk of magnesia
- 1 tube of antiseptic cream
- 1 tube of bug bite cream
- 1 packet of assorted size Band-Aids

Important notes and tips on using medicines for children:

- Always read the label before giving medicine to a child.
- Make sure that your child isn't allergic to the medicine or any of its ingredients.
- Never give a child more medicine than the recommended dose.
- Ibuprofen and acetaminophen may be taken at the same time.
- If you are worried about the health of your child, look online for help, talk to a pharmacist for advice, or contact your doctor.

▶

If you are looking after your child on your own and your child is taking a course of medicine such as antibiotics, then make sure you understand the regime and follow it exactly. Take notes if necessary. Interrupting a course of medicine at the very least will considerably reduce its efficacy and can seriously harm your child. If your child is ill and has been given any over-the-counter medicines like ibuprofen or acetaminophen that day, find out when the last dose was given. Painkillers are dangerous if given more frequently than every four hours, so when you take over, it is important to establish these details. If you give your child any medicines while you're in charge, then when mom comes back, remember to tell her exactly what they took and when; write it down so there is no confusion. Do not rely on your child to remember, as children have a different perception of time.

2 Keep some simple emergency medicines in your car

Nowadays, we spend a significant amount of time in the car. Be prepared to manage minor illness and headaches wherever you are. Having a few things handy can save the day on that special outing. The car is an easy thing to stock up. Buy wet wipes, some plastic cutlery, and a roll of toilet paper, put them in a duffel bag and keep them in the trunk. Buy some antiseptic cream and Band-Aids as on the previous list, one packet of children's acetaminophen, a few ibuprofen syrup packets, and some children's chewable antacid tablets. Always make a note of the time you give your child a painkiller so that you will not inadvertently give another dose too soon.

3 Get a set of colored felt pens, small paper scissors, and sticky tape

Kids love coloring and drawing, and whether just sitting at home or going somewhere by car or train, having crayons and plain paper handy for them to use is a lifesaver. You don't have to get expensive markers, but bright-colored and washable ones are a must. Check them regularly or watch while your children use them. When they start running out, replace them. They're not expensive, and most supermarkets sell them. Remember how you used to love new markers when you were a kid, and how boring it was when every pen you picked up was on the way out?

4 Plan enough time into your schedule for meals

When you're in charge of your children and doing exciting things, it is easy to lose track of the time and forget to prepare a meal or eat properly. When kids get hungry their behavior deteriorates, which can spoil the day. Make sure that you have planned what and when you're going to eat.

5 Buy some small Tupperware boxes so that you can freeze extra food you cook

When you cook for your kids, always make more than you need and freeze the spare. Use either cheap Tupperware boxes or any small, plastic packaging pots. These are ideal for freezing the extra food in single-serving portions and perfect for you to microwave another day when you don't feel like cooking or time is short.

Freeze sliced bread

When you have a busy lifestyle, always having the right food can be tricky. Food like bread can easily become stale before you have had a chance to eat it. If you freeze sliced bread, it keeps indefinitely. You can toast frozen bread straight from the freezer and make great packed lunch or picnic sandwiches from it while it is still frozen because, being hard, butter spreads on it easily. When you've made your sandwiches, wrap them immediately in foil or saran wrap and then in 10 minutes or less the bread will be defrosted and fresh. Plus, if you wrap the sandwiches and put them in your insulated lunch box, they help keep the rest of the food cool until lunchtime.

Take small bottles of tap water with you when you go out

Kids get thirsty and you should always make sure that they have enough water to drink, especially on hot days, so save a few plastic bottles, fill them with tap water, and take them with you. This will save you filling up on canned soda drinks and it's much cheaper. Always keep a full one in the car.

Freeze single-serving juice cartons

Great for packed lunches and picnics; the frozen drink slowly defrosts in the cooler bag, keeping everything nice and cold, then by lunchtime it will be ready to drink.

Buy a simple tool kit

May be your dad had one, maybe he didn't, but a small tool kit will be very useful and is something you should get. Superglue and two-part resin are perfect for mending broken toys and so are useful things for a dad to have around. Children should never be allowed to use superglue, though. Ideally you will need:

- A small screwdriver set
- A small flashlight
- A pair of strong kitchen scissors
- A roll of sticky tape
- 1 tube cyanoacrylate glue (superglue)
- 1 pair of tubes of two-part resin glue.

Buy a basic making kit

This book is about how you can do things with your kids. One of the most rewarding things you can do, for both you and your kids, is to make stuff with them. You don't need any equipment to start because some of the projects only require a piece of paper, but for about $30, you can set yourself up with some basic equipment that will enable you to make the most fantastic toys and models from just about any old junk around the house.

feather quill PAGE 144 magical ink pot PAGE 148

When I was a boy of fourteen, my father was so ignorant I could hardly stand to have the old man around. But when I got to be twenty-one, I was astonished at how much the old man had learned in seven years.

MARK TWAIN
Character of Samuel Clemens, author

WAVES AND WHEELS

helicopter PAGE 103

formula one racing car PAGE 99

steam train PAGE 110

floating container ship

Bathtime means perfect conditions for this ship's journey

One of the quickest models to put together, this floating container ship is made from a couple of old dishwasher or washing machine liquid bottles and a few other bits and pieces. It's not even sprayed, but plenty of fun was had making and playing with it. When it was made, my kids loved naming it in permanent marker, and then sailing it across the great Bath Ocean.

8 years +

40 minutes

Glue gun
Marker
Craft knife
Large dishwasher soap bottle
Small dishwasher soap bottle
Piece of cardboard
Shower gel bottle
2l milk carton cap
Liquid detergent bottle cap
Yogurt cup base

**A FEW
SMALL
STONES**

1 To make a floating ship, you'll need a plastic bottle for the hull. Use a detergent bottle. Mark a line round the bottle using a permanent marker. Cut the hull from a large bottle and the cabin from a smaller bottle.

4 Cut some small supports at the right height to allow the deck to be slightly recessed. Glue these to the underside of the deck. Glue round the edge of the deck and slide in. Glue the milk bottle top into the detergent bottle opening. To stop your ship from being top heavy, glue a few small stones inside the hull before you glue the deck into position.

2 Place hull part upside down on a piece of thick cardboard and draw around it with a marker.

GLUE

5 With deck in place, glue around it to make sure it's waterproof.

3 Cut out the deck slightly inside the line so that the cardboard will just fit inside the hull.

6 Glue the cabin upside down to the deck, then glue the yogurt cup end to the deck.

7 Cut the end off a shower gel pack and glue to the front of the cabin to make the bridge. Glue a detergent bottle top to the top of the bridge to make a funnel.

8 Decorate with marker, then play with it in the bathtub!

TIP: Let your children name the ship and launch it down the slope at the end of the bathtub.

floating submarine

One evening as bathtime approached, there was a distinct lack of new and exciting bath toys. "Dad, can you make something for us to play with in the bath? Something that's really cool and really works?"

I rescued an empty soda bottle from the bin and armed with that, an empty trigger-spray bathroom cleaner bottle, a glue gun, and a can of gray undercoat, we started to make our first-ever junk model. This sub looks the part and really floats. To get the right effect, it's partially filled with stones, sand, or gravel from the garden. I dried it out in the oven quickly to sterilize it and stop it from going moldy.

Safety first: When making this kind of toy, make sure that containers are thoroughly washed out, no bits can fall off, and that there are no sharp corners. Never give a plastic toy you have made to a child under three years of age.

A very easy and quick way to make a great bath toy that really floats

8 years +

40 minutes

Glue gun
Marker
Craft knife
Paint
Plastic soda bottle
Trigger-spray bottle neck

floating submarine

1 Remove bottle cap and keep; cut off tamper evident ring and discard.

2 Glue single-serving dessert cup to bottle bottom. If the pot has a lip, cut off with a pair of strong kitchen scissors or a craft knife so that pot makes a neat, rounded end to the squash bottle. Make sure that glue goes completely around edge of pot so that the pot is sealed on to the end of the bottle, otherwise water will seep into pot when the submarine is finished and being played with in the bath.

3 Glue deodorant bottle cap to end of dessert cup to make the submarine prow.

4 To make coning tower, cut the top part from a kitchen or bathroom pump spray. Use strong kitchen scissors. Mark a straight line on each side and a slightly curved line on the front and back so that the tower will sit nicely on the bottle.

5 Glue the coning tower to the top of the main hull, making sure that if there are any features in the side of the squash bottle, they are aligned to be horizontal and symmetrical.

6 Glue a milk bottle cap to the top of the coning tower so that it is hanging slightly more to the front, to make a deck.

7 To make the tail fins, using any spare flat piece of bottle plastic, trace the profile of the bottle with a marker. To match profile, hold pen vertically and look down from the top. Mark out the shape of the fin and cut out using strong scissors. Cut rounded corners so that fins don't scratch.

8 Using another spare bit of flat plastic bottle side, mark a 7 cm diameter circle using a cup or compass, **A**. Draw around the bottle cap, **B**. Draw around the bottle neck, **C**, making sure the circles are concentric.

9 Cut out the disc using strong scissors, although you may need a craft knife to get the inner circle started.

10 Mark eight radial spokes that only go as far as circle **B**.

11 Using strong scissors, cut down each spoke two-thirds of the way around each segment on circle **B**. These are the propeller blades, do not cut them off.

12 Twist and bend out each blade in turn, creasing the plastic to make it stay bent.

floating submarine

13 In order to float at the correct depth and upright, the sub needs ballast. Half fill the submarine with sand or gravel.

14 Push propeller onto bottle neck and replace cap tightly, but do not glue. Cap can be removed to add or remove ballast at later date. Because propeller is not glued, it will be able to rotate.

15 Glue the tail fins in place, making sure that they are horizontal and level with each other. Glue any other pieces of old plastic or bottle caps to the surface of the submarine hull to add detail as required.

16 Decorate with any suitable waterproof paint. Use spray paint if you have it because it dries quickly, which means that you can get on and play with the sub in the bath.

Why not give the sub a number that is special to you and your children, like your house number or their ages, and paint it on the side?

formula one racing car

Do you recognize the kitchen-cleaner bottle? Perhaps it's the special new formula they're using these days, but this container makes a brilliant racing car. The wheels work, the car really rolls, and it also fits a small action figure. We didn't have time to spray ours because the race was about to start, but no doubt you will plan your day better, and then you'll have time to adorn it with all manner of sponsors' logos and advertising, just like the real thing.

This Formula One racer cleans up and really rolls

8 years +
1 hour

Glue gun
Marker
Craft knife
Paint
kitchen-cleaner
   bottle
1 L or 2 L milk
   bottle caps
Piece of cardboard
Drinking straws
Tiny piece of packing-
   foam sheet
Piece of clear plastic
   bottle
Pen caps or
   chocolate box tray

formula one racing car

1 Carefully mark the cut lines, making sure that the axle holes are in line so that the axles will be at right angles to the bottle's long axis and will be parallel.

Mark a slot, **A**, as deep as the thick cardboard you are going to use.

4 To make the wheels, you will need eight milk bottle caps. Cut square holes or drill only four of the caps in the center.

GLUE

2 Cut square holes or drill holes for the axles just a little bit bigger than a drinking straw. Cut a slit at the bottom of each hole so you can get the axle/wheels assemblies in.

3 Only cut a C shape for the cockpit so you can bend the bottle down to make the seat back.

5 Glue a straw onto the underside of the undrilled cap, making sure that it is central and straight.

When the glue has set, pass a drilled cap over the straw and glue around the rim.

formula one racing car

6 Offer the wheel up to the car body and mark the correct length of the straw. Allowing for the other wheel, cut the straw to length and repeat steps 4 and 5 for the other wheel. Repeat for the second axle.

7 Cut a piece of thick cardboard to fit the slot **A** and form the floor of the car and the bottom of the side fuel tank bulge.

GLUE

A

8 Fold down the cockpit flap and glue to the floor to make seat and seat back.

9 Snap fit axle/wheel assemblies into place.

10 Cut a piece of thick cardboard to make the front spoiler, upper parts of the fuel tank, side bulges, and wing mirrors and glue in to place.

11 Cut a crescent-shaped windshield from a piece of clear soda bottle and glue around cockpit front.

12 To make engine, use a piece of chocolate box tray or some old pen caps stuck on a piece of cardboard, markered or sprayed black.

13 For the exhaust pipes, cut six short pieces from some drinking straws and stick in two rows on the top of the engine block.

14 Glue a tiny piece of packing foam to the front of the engine as a headrest.

15 To make the rear spoiler, cut thick cardboard into two identical short strips and angle tops. Glue to side of body. **NOTE:** You might need a cardboard spacer, depending on the size of the engine part.

16 Cut a rectangle of cardboard to make the rear spoiler and glue on top of the uprights. Glue a strip of paper to the pieces of cardboard on the top and bottom of the fuel tank bulge to complete. Color the cardboard bits and take the wheels off and spray them black if you want a more authentic look.

Look on the web for graphics on real formula one cars and copy the designs onto your model.

helicopter

This is a nice, complicated model for when you have a whole afternoon to occupy. The main rotor turns, and the wire coathanger skid-supports flex really nicely when you land it.

You probably won't have exactly the same containers as we did, but making a model from junk is all about discovery, improvisation, problem solving, and working with what is available. With a model like this, you most likely find you are doing most of the work, but your kids will love finding suitable things for the next bit you are making, or suggesting solutions when stuff doesn't look right.

Some of the ideas in this project will be helpful whatever type of chopper you make; the way the rotor is put together, how to make a decent-looking tail, how to make the skids—the rest, however, is up to you. The main thing is to start with something nice and chunky for the body and attach the rest onto that.

Make this superb helicopter —it's satisfyingly big and the main rotors turn

14 years +
4 hours

Glue gun
Marker
Craft knife
Paint
Cardboard
Coathanger
Pliers
Assorted bottles and
   tubs

helicopter

1 Choose a carton or make a box that fits the width of a kitchen-cleaner bottle.

5 Cut a segment out of a washing-liquid ball and glue gun to the end of the kitchen-cleaner bottle.

GLUE

2 Cut a kitchen-cleaner bottle in half and glue gun it into the bottom of the open end of the box.

6 To make the tail, cut a toilet paper roll lengthwise and roll it down thinner, to make a slight cone. Glue gun it together and then glue on to single-portion dessert cup at a slight angle.

3 Glue a single-portion dessert cup on the end of the box.

GLUE

4 Cut the top off a clear salad or dips package and insert it into gap at top of open end of main carton body, then glue onto kitchen-cleaner bottle.

7 To make skis, use two pieces of cardboard. Bend them up in a curve and glue them together for added strength and so that they stay curved.

helicopter

GLUE

8 Using pliers, bend two pieces of coathanger to form the undercarriage and glue gun them to the skis.

11 To make the main rotor, cut rotor blades from a piece of cardboard, and glue coathanger wire through a bottle top so that it can rotate. Poke wire through rotor, cover end of wire with a cut-down pen cap. Glue coathanger wire strips from top of rotor to pen cap. Glue whole assembly to dessert top.

9 Put more glue-gun glue over the wires and cover the ends with small pieces of slightly curved cardboard to make a really firm fixture.

GLUE

10 Glue the main body of the helicopter to the top of the undercarriage, making sure that it is level as the glue sets (glue-gun glue will take up to 60 seconds to set).

12 To make the tail rotor assembly, cut rotor from a piece of cardboard, glue it to a 2 L-milk carton lid, and glue the assembled part onto tail. Cut stabilizing fin from cardboard and glue at right angles to the tail on the opposite side. Cap the end of the tail with a sliced-off bottle cap.

13 Glue rotor assembly to top of main body.

▶

14 To make the engines, slit a toilet paper roll lengthwise then cut in half, roll up tighter, and glue with glue gun. Cap one end with a single-portion bottle cap, crumple wrapping paper or tin foil, and glue in the other end. Glue the assembly to a milk carton lid. Make two of these.

16 Cut single-portion, dessert-cup bottle in half lengthwise and stick one-half on each side of the main body. Glue other pieces of plastic, strips, or small bits to various parts of the helicopter to add detail.

17 Finally, paint your model. If you use spray paint, it is a good idea to mask the cockpit windscreen with a bit of masking tape or sticky tape. Once it is painted, decorate further with a black permanent marker.

 15 Glue engines to top of main body just behind the rotor assembly. If you have a wider body or longer engines, they can go on either side of the rotor assembly.

TIP: Paint some of the components before assembling them to get a really good effect.

canoe

It looks the part, fits a small action figure, and I only wish it fit me! I hear canoes are quite expensive, but this one certainly wasn't.

This is the sort of model that you can make in a few minutes when the kids are bored and want something to do. In essence it is very, very simple, because it is made out of two shower gel bottles glued together, neck to neck. A couple of little bits of detail finish it off, like the splash-guard and the seat, but really this is a ten- to twenty- minute project. Next time you buy shower gel, shampoo or conditioner, have a look at all the bottle shapes offered. All you need for this project is a bottle that stands on its cap, is vaguely symmetrical, and has a rounded end. It's not rocket science … it's junk model-making canoe science!

A canoe made from two shower gel bottles; what could be more perfect for the bath?

8 years +

1 hour

Glue gun
Marker
Craft knife
Paint
2 x shower gel
  bottles
Shampoo or
  conditioner bottle
Plastic bottle
Styrofoam fruit tray
Wooden coffee
  stirrers or lollipop
  sticks
OPTIONAL:
Short piece of string
  or bootlace

canoe

4 Remove sticky tape, separate pieces, and cut cockpit opening in each half.

1 To make the canoe, you will need two shower gel bottles with simple tapered or rounded ends. Remove caps, mark, and then cut off the bottle tops so that about ½ cm of the shoulder remains on one of them but not on the other. You will use this to make a strong joint when you glue the ends together.

5 Cut the base from an expanded styrofoam fruit tray and glue into one-half of the canoe, making sure to leave room at the bottom edge for the other half of the canoe and shoulder to fit in.

2 Without glue, push the ends together and hold in place with sticky tape.

3 To make the splash guard deck top, cut the top shoulder from an oval shampoo or hair conditioner bottle (or something similar) that is no wider than the shower gel bottles you are using. Tape in place, and using as a guide, mark the size of the cockpit opening.

6 Apply glue around the shoulder ridge and push both ends of the canoe together. If you are unsure that you have a watertight joint, wait till the glue has set (60 seconds) and then apply a bead of glue round the joint from the outside.

canoe

7 Glue the splash guard deck over the cockpit opening to finish off neatly (optional).

8 Make the paddle from coffee stirrers or lollipop sticks with a small piece of brightly colored plastic bottle cut to paddle shape, glued at each end.

9 Name, decorate with marker pen, and spray if required.

TIP: Find a typeface you like, print the words on A4 paper, and then copy them onto the model with permanent marker.

steam train

A magnificent wood-burning steam locomotive with real rolling wheels

12 years +

2 hours

Bottle caps
Thick and thin cardboard
Coathanger wire
Glue-gun glue (ideally)
Set of compasses
Single-serving drink bottle
Black and one-color paint (ideally spray paint)

Looking every inch like something that you'd buy from an expensive toy shop, this beautiful train is as satisfying to make as it is fun to play with.

These instructions include templates to trace over for the basic chassis and the cabin as well as measurements for all the important parts. However, given that this model is made from junk, you'll also have to use your inventiveness where your parts aren't exactly the same as mine. That said, don't limit yourself to what junk packaging you have left over in the cupboard. If you want to start this project but you haven't collected the right bottles and lids, just buy the ones you want next time you go to the supermarket—that way you can get exactly the bottle shape and size you need. The best products for shape are personal care and bath products, shower gels, and soap-dispensing bottles.

Be adventurous—have a go at making this wonderful model, perfect for hours of fun and enjoyment.

steam train

NOTE: When starting a model, the scale is one of the hardest things to judge, especially when you are using junk components. As your parts may differ from the ones used for this model, use these templates, and the dimensions given in the project, as a guide.

front-wheel truck
TEMPLATE

cabin side wall
TEMPLATE **x 2**

cabin front wall TEMPLATE

rear-wheel truck TEMPLATE

steam train

1   For this project, you will need four large wheels and four small ones. For the large wheels, use poly-bottle milk lids with diameter 1½ in (or similar), and for the small wheels, use fizzy drink bottle lids, diameter 1 in. Draw four circles at 2 in diameter. On four at 4 cm diameter, on some thick cardboard (foamboard is perfect). Cut out and then glue the lids centrally, one to each disc.

If you don't have any bottle caps, you can cut the middle disc of each wheel out of the same cardboard.

2   Like real train wheels, this is a fixed-axle design. Cut four lengths of straight coat-hanger wire about 8½ cm long. To make each wheel pair, push one end of a wire length through the cardboard side of the wheel. Remove it and then put the nozzle of the glue gun up to the hole and squeeze in a little bit of glue-gun glue. Push the wire axle in fully.

3   Do the same at the other end of the wire so that you have two wheels glued securely on the axle. Make sure that the wheels are at right angles to each other. Repeat for the other big and small wheels until you have four sets of wheels and axles.

USE TEMPLATE

4   To make the wheel trucks, cut two sets of two rectangular pieces of thick cardboard. The width of the cardboard should just fit between the wheels so that they don't rub. The width will depend on the size of lid you used for the wheels and the thickness of your cardboard. In one small bit and one large bit, make two crosswise channels (spaced apart as shown). Either cut a V-shaped groove or crush the cardboard in with the back of a dinner knife. Do no cut all the way through. Only make grooves in one set of the rectangles.

5 Carefully glue around the parts with the grooves in, making sure not to get the glue in the grooves, and then rest the wheel assemblies in the grooves and stick the matching bits of cardboard over the top. This will trap the wheel assemblies but still allow them to rotate freely.

7 Now that you have the basic running-gear assembly, you can start to build up the locomotive parts. Cut two long, thin rectangles of thick cardboard that extend to just cover the big wheels and glue them onto the top of the chassis. Cut four, small rectangles of thick cardboard and glue them behind the big wheels (these will be the driver's steps). Use two on each side. Finally, cut a piece of thin cardboard only as wide as the chassis and use it to box in the part over the small wheels.

6 Join the two wheel trucks with thick cardboard, shaped as shown. Cut two rectangles of thick cardboard about 25 cm long and about 6 cm wide. Rest the wheels on a level surface and cut a step in the cardboard so that you can glue it to both sets of wheels. Make sure that when the cardboard is glued to the base, it stands higher than the big wheels. To do this, the width of the cardboard at the big-wheel end should not be less than 3 cm, although its actual size depends on the size of wheels that you have chosen.

8 Spray the whole assembly black. Don't spray too thickly all at once, or you will gum up the wheels. Three or four light coats of spray from all angles should be enough, making sure that the wheels still turn after each coat.

▶

9 Use a large, straight-sided, personal care or soap-pump-dispenser bottle for the boiler. If you don't have the right one at home, buy a cheap one and decant the contents into another bottle. Mark around the bottle so that your cut will be at right angles to the axis of the bottle and neatly cut with strong scissors.

GLUE

10 To make the funnel, mark then cut the top and base off a single-serving drink bottle. At the top, cut slightly past the shoulder so that the top fits snugly in the base part. Turn over, apply glue to the cut rim of the top, and glue inside the base. When set, carefully cut a circular hole from the base part to make the funnel opening. **Take care**; the base of a bottle is the toughest part of the plastic, and it is easy to slip and cut yourself if you are pressing hard.

11 Rest the boiler onto the wheel chassis and position the funnel in the best place and carefully mark around it on the boiler.

12 Carefully cut out the hole for the funnel base. Check that the funnel fits and adjust the hole as necessary. You'll see that the top of the bottle that you used for the funnel has a flange around it; this will form a nice finish when the funnel is inserted. Apply glue to the funnel and push into the hole in the top of the boiler.

13 Glue a smaller-rounded bottle cap in place behind the funnel and then paint the boiler and funnel. Spray is best, and if you used clear bottles, spray inside for a lovely, glossy finish.

USE TEMPLATE

14 Make the lamp from three small rectangular pieces of thick cardboard glued together. For a neat finish, cover the edges with thin cardboard or paper and paint or spray the finished block black. To make the light, cut a thin slice off the top of a white or clear single-serving drink bottle and glue to the block.

x2

15 Make two drive pistons, one for each side, using a rolled-up piece of thin cardboard or plastic glued at each end into a single-serving drink bottle cap. Paint or spray the same color as the boiler.

16 Glue the boiler and drive pistons in place, so that the pistons are level with the front of the boiler and rest up against the front of the walk-boards. Glue the lamp in place. Cut the cabin out of thick cardboard using the templates as a guide. For a neat finish, paint the cabin before you glue it to the locomotive assembly.

Use a piece of thin cardboard for the curved roof, cut out so that it overhangs by a small amount at the front and sides and as far as the back of the locomotive at the back. Lastly, use thin cardboard to make the cabin floor to fit inside the cabin; paint and glue in place.

17 Add detail and decorate as much as you want. Stick black straws to the sides of the boiler as guide rails and at the joint between the boiler and chassis to hide any glue blobs. Stick thin pieces of cardboard to the cabin side as trim and anything else you can think of.

Now why not make some carriages to go with your motive . . . Choo choo!

Egg timer

Accurately measure time using sand and two drink bottles

Nowadays, hourglasses are used almost entirely for decorative purposes because much more accurate ways of measuring time have been invented. Nevertheless, this great little experiment results in a durable and dynamic model that is as fascinating to watch as it is fun to build and talk about.

12 years +

2 hours

Single-serving drink bottles
Small piece of plastic
Fine sand
Sandpaper

People have been using the flow of sand to measure the passing hours of the day since the time of the Egyptians. From about the fifteenth century onward, sand-filled hourglasses were being used by just about anybody who could afford one.

During Magellan's pioneering voyage to circumnavigate the world, each ship kept as many as eighteen hourglasses, and it was the job of a ship's page to turn the hourglasses to provide times for the ship's log. In this project, you'll see how easy it is to make a sand timer that can be used to accurately measure the time needed to boil an egg. Use soft, fine, dry sand, calibrate your timer carefully, and it will accurately measure the three minutes it takes to cook a perfect soft-boiled egg.

Building an egg timer combines proper science with all the fun of a making project your kids can have an active role in. On page 121, you'll find an experimental discussion outline with a few key interesting facts designed to help boost your children's interest and simply explain what's going on in the experiment.

1 Drill a small hole (about 1 mm to 2 mm in diameter, depending on the grade of sand you're using) in the center of the bottle cap. Use a cordless drill and hold the cap carefully, preferably in a small vice.

2 To calibrate your timer, fill the bottle with sand and screw on the cap with the hole in it and time how long it takes for all the sand to drain out. Add more sand to make it last longer or drill a bigger hole to make it go quicker, until it takes three minutes to drain out.

3 Put the sand to one side and saw off the threaded part of the bottle just above the shoulder ring. You will need to do this for both bottles. Make sure that the shoulder ring is flat and level. Sandpaper the surface lightly to smooth it off and give a key for the glue.

4 Draw around the shoulder of one of the bottles with a marker onto a piece of thin packaging plastic cut from a detergent bottle or something similar.

5 Holding the plastic sheet carefully, drill a hole in the center of the drawn circle using the same diameter drill bit as the one you calibrated with in step 2. (Make sure to drill into a piece of scrap wood and not your tabletop). Cut out the circle of plastic and sandpaper both sides.

▶

6 Fill one of the bottles with the exact amount of sand from your calibration in step 2.

7 Use quick-setting epoxy glue or glue-gun glue around the top of the shoulder of one bottle.

8 Carefully stick the circle of plastic onto the shoulder, making sure that no glue goes inside the bottle or the hole.

9 When the first layer of glue is set, repeat and stick the other bottle upside down onto the first bottle. Be very careful to make sure that the bottle joints are sealed and the glue does not flow into the hole.

Experimental discussion

When was the first recorded use of a sand timer?

The earliest pictures showing the use of the hourglass seems to be in the AD 1338 fresco *Allegory of Good Government* by Ambrogio Lorenzetti.

What is the largest sand timer in the world?

Since 2008, the largest sand timer in the world has been in Red Square in Moscow. It stands nearly 12 meters in height, weighs 40 tons and can run for over a year on one turn!

Are sand timers still used in public?

Apart from loads of people using them for fun to time egg boiling and as simple timers in board games, both houses of the Australian Parliament still use three hourglasses to time certain procedures, such as divisions (the time taken to take a vote on a question).

What is an hourglass figure?

The shape of the hourglass with its bulge at top and bottom and a narrow part in the middle gave its name to the look of the painful corset worn by women to give them a silhouette resembling the hourglass shape: wide bottom, narrow waist, and wide top.

Reliable routines

As we get older, we are told that routine is something to avoid, a numbing thing that saps our creativity, stifles our energy and will dull our luster if we let it. But like it or not, routine is something that we all need a bit of. It is the framework that provides us with the security to step out and be creative when we want to. For kids, life without routine is very frightening and confusing. Routines act as a cushion for the hustle and bustle of growing up in a family and provide a set of reliable reference points for everyone involved.

Dads are good at starting routines, the best of which grow into family traditions or etch themselves into our memories as happy times we spent together. Whilst always being ready to be creative and mix things up a bit, never forget the importance of the routines you set up, keep the important ones; your children will cherish them dearly.

Here are some routines that will hopefully inspire you and give you ideas about things to do with your children to show them that whatever happens they can always rely on you.

1 Be part of their bedtime routine

Help set up and be a regular part of their evening routine and especially when they are young, stick religiously to it. Make an extra effort to be home from work in time to put your kids to bed, even if it is only on certain days. If you are away from home for any reason make time to call home at this time to say goodnight to them. Wherever you are, don't forget to do it so your children can rely on speaking to you and knowing that you are alright before they go to sleep.

2 Buy a bun

Go to the bakery to pick up a treat for the kids on your way back from picking them up from school on the same day each week or at the same time in the morning on the weekend.

The smell of fresh bread is lovely and everything feels great when you have some food inside you. If you don't live near a bakery, buy hot cross buns at the supermarket and toast them at the same time each weekend.

3 Have and play a favorite tape, CD, or iPod playlist in the car

Choose tracks with your children or let them pick their favorite ones that you can all sing along to. Make sure that they are upbeat songs.

4 Always make the same favorite meal on the same day of the week

Make sure it is a healthy and tasty meal that your children like and then you know that they will look forward to it.

5 Make a mealtime routine

Whether it is breakfast or dinner everyday, or if due to work commitments it can only be done on the weekend, make time to sit down with your children while you share a meal. It's a great opportunity for you to hear their banter and find out what's been going on in their lives and it gives you an opportunity to act as a team when they help set the table or clear away the dishes with you.

6 Do homework with your children each week

At first this might seem like a chore, but get it right and you'll find yourself spending some real quality time with your children as you sit with them and help them through their homework. Not only do you get to see what they are doing at school, but you get to help them get better grades.

7 Set aside one special night every month as a home film night

Rent out that old favorite or the latest release, get a bar of chocolate or some popcorn and make a fun routine out of it. The key is to set aside a regular spot that you don't let work or other commitments get in the way.

8 Read to your children at bedtime

Cozy in their beds, warm, happy, relaxed and listening to their dad read them a story, what kid could ask for more? What a lovely routine to look forward to. Get into a good book and you'll be looking forward to the next chapter as much as they do.

9 Set up a birthday routine

Routines don't have to be just about what you do each week, yearly routines are just as important. Set up a nice birthday routine, a restaurant meal, or a special celebratory trip out. Make it a thing you can do each year, and stick to it. Next year will come around soon enough, and before you know it you will have a wonderful birthday tradition to look forward to.

10 Set up a Christmas time tradition

Some of our most enduring memories are from the holidays we spent together with our families when we were young. A Christmas, or special holiday season tradition can give your children something to pass on to their kids. There are many traditions that you can set up having to do with food, decorating and present giving, but here are some ideas to help you create that special festive routine:

Keep the decorations and Christmas tree lights in the same box in the attic or garage and each year make a point of getting them out with your kids and write the year on the side of the box in marker pen.

Make a Christmas stocking with your children and decorate it with their initials. Keep them carefully from year to year and get them out on Christmas Eve to hang at the end of their beds or on the fireplace mantelpiece.

Plan to make a photo album or photobook of the festivities. There are some very good online services that let you to lay out a book with your own scans or digital photographs and then print it, bind it and mail it to you. Taking the photos is the obvious part, but making special routine out of laying out the book together at the end of the festivities is a great way to finish up the holiday. Over the years the growing set of books you create will be a wonderful thing to get out with your children and reminisce over as they grow up.

steam train PAGE 110

I cannot think of any need in childhood as strong as the need for a father's protection.

DR SIGMUND FREUD
Father of psychology

GREAT ADVENTURES

Children don't need much to fire up their imaginations and are desperate to participate in the fictional universes of their favorite game and story characters. These Great Adventures projects play to this need by adding imaginary backstories to each plan, turning the projects into voyages of discovery, and providing a starting point for the richest possible interaction with each craft activity.

dragonhide valuables pouch PAGE 127

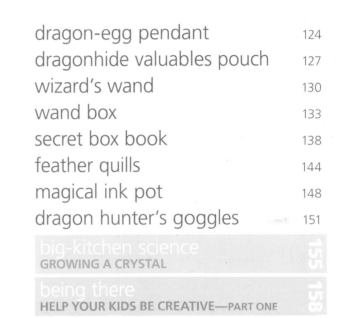

feather quills PAGE 144

dragon hunter's goggles PAGE 151

dragon-egg pendant

Hide your dragon's eggs from prying eyes

8 years +

45 minutes
(incl. glue drying)

Dowel pins
Hacksaw
Paint (that dries
waterproof)
Small metal
screw eye
Sandpaper
Glue-gun glue

Each morning after breakfast, I set aside two hours to attend to my mail pile. Never a day goes by when I am not somehow transported to a distant realm by the opening of an envelope. On one such occasion, I received a letter from an experienced explorer called Melros. The letter contained four miniature dragon's eggs, which, although harmless-looking enough, had caused her considerable problems. Melros had disguised them as pendants, but when that failed to stop unwanted interest, she sent them to me for safe keeping.

An hour or two in the library revealed that these were extremely rare and fine examples of petrified Wisp Dragon eggs. As I know how interested you are in such diversions, I hereby provide you the instructions needed to make replicas so that you can own one or two of these exquisite pieces for yourself. They make charming pendants and will never fail to elicit a comment or two from admirers each time they are worn.

dragon-egg pendant

1 Use 10- to 12mm dowel and mark about 2½ cm lengths for each minidragon's egg you want to make.

2 Use a hacksaw to saw the dowel to length (hold the longer end). This is good sawing practice for kids as it is easy and safe to use a hacksaw.

3 Sandpaper the corners off to make the ends rounded like an egg.

4 Screw a small metal eye into the center of one end. It might help to make a small hole to start with, using a nail.

5 Holding the metal eye, apply a thin trickle of glue-gun glue in an organic pattern over the surface of the egg.

6 Put sticky tape either side of the metal eye as a mask and a handle and paint the egg in your chosen color with waterproof paint.

dragon-egg pendant

 7 To distress, paint on a layer of darker acrylic thinned with water.

9 When dry, carefully paint silver or gold paint on the glue-gun lines.

10 Thread onto a necklace chain gold thread or yarn to make an attractive necklace.

 8 Before the paint dries, wipe off with a cloth, leaving some paint in the cracks.

Wear your pendant when you go out and you are guaranteed admiring glances—but be careful of those Wisp Dragons; they want their eggs back!

dragonhide valuables pouch

Dragonhide is a remarkable material; its surface hardness is comparable to that of quartz, and in the past it was rendered workable only with specialist tools tipped with topaz, corundum, or diamond. In the late nineteenth century, centers capable of tanning dragonhide existed in a few countries, but if one desired the most superb workmanship, material of the highest quality, and security of supply, then only the tanneries in Mongolia's capital, the City of Felt, would suffice.

Apparently, dragonhide is still widely available, and these days, equipment exists that permits you to make accessories like this exquisite pouch. I have had Collinworth draw up some simple instructions, which I'm certain you will be able to follow, should the mood take you.

Once the top of this valuables pouch is pulled shut, only the nimblest fingers will be able to loosen the cord, thus it will keep all manner of treasure safe from theft and misadventure.

A magnificent dragonhide accessory that will keep all your valuables safe

10 years +

15 minutes

Scissors
Glue gun
Soft fabric
String or cord

dragonhide valuables pouch

1 Cut out a rectangle of velour, felt, or velvet fabric about 30 cm by 10 cm.

2 Fold the fabric over face-side in and cut about four small scallops out of the cut edge. Mark a line across the fabric to get the hole positions neatly aligned.

3 Fold the fabric over at the marked line and cut out four small holes by cutting semicircles across the fold. Repeat at the other end.

4 Place face up and put a thin stripe of glue-gun glue as close to the edge as you can, halfway down both sides (as shown).

5 Fold the fabric over, making certain to keep it square, and flatten out. Wait for two minutes until the glue has cooled and set.

6 Turn the bag right-side out and then carefully dribble glue-gun glue stripes diagonally across the fabric surface. Crisscross them to give a diamond pattern. Do both sides the same.

dragonhide valuables pouch

7 When the glue has set, either paint gold onto the glue strips or use antique finger nail polish to highlight the glue stripes. You can use silver, any metallic paint, or even black if you don't have gold.

8 Thread cord or elastic braid through the holes, in for the first hole and then out and in till you have gone all around the neck of the bag. Tie off the cord in a simple knot.

9 Using another piece of the same cord, thread through in the same fashion but start from the other side.

Now when you pull the two knotted ends apart, the bag should close tightly.

If it doesn't stay closed, you may have to thread the cords back on themselves one more time.

TIP: The perfect carrying case for your valuables, or even your glasses.

wizard's wand

Cast a craft spell as you make this wonderful wand

12 years +	
60 minutes (incl. glue drying)	
A4 paper sheet Double-sided tape Glue gun PVA	

Of all the magical instruments, none is considered as important or as useful to the budding witch or wizard as the wand. The more conservative members of the magical community would have us believe that only those most skilled in the craft of wandmaking can fashion a wand. But having seen a wandsman at work, I have concluded that anyone should easily be able to make a beautiful wand capable of the most powerful magic.

Another myth I would like to dispel without further ado is the outdated idea that each wizard or witch may only possess one wand. Some of the world's finest sorcerers, a few of whom I have known personally, have any number of wands, each one capable of a particular form of magic. I knew one eminent spellbinder whose prized wand collection numbered 366, one for each day of the year, including a priceless golden *toverstokje* only to be used on that most magical of days, February 29th.

wizard's wand

1 Stick a strip of double-sided tape diagonally across a sheet of A4 paper.

2 Roll the paper up very tightly diagonally, allowing one end to be slightly less tight than the other to give a thin tapered roll.

PVA GLUE

3 When you roll over the double-sided tape, stop and put a little PVA (white glue) on the remaining paper.

4 Roll tightly and leave to dry for 30 minutes.

5 Trim to give straight ends.

6 Fill each end with glue-gun glue (one end at a time). Pack the big end with tissue paper if you want to use less glue. The big end may take a couple of goes to plug it completely.

7 Turn the wand while applying a glue-gun bead to make a nice pattern. Keep turning while it sets (about a minute).

▶

wizard's wand

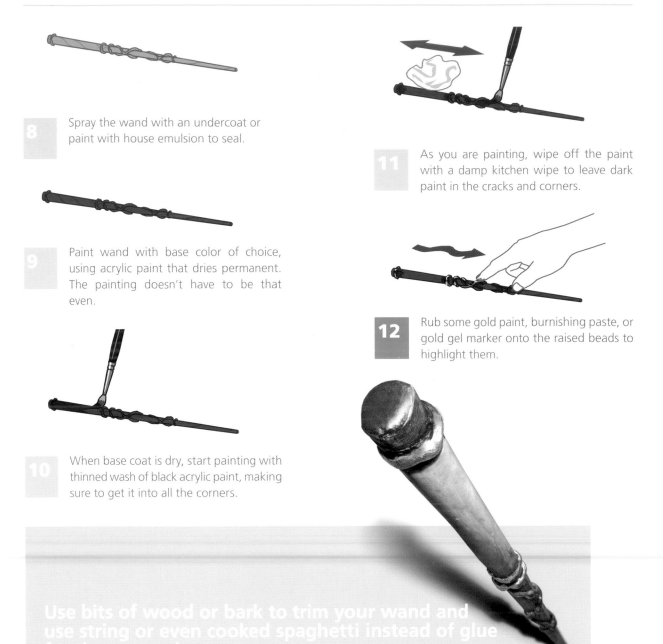

8 Spray the wand with an undercoat or paint with house emulsion to seal.

9 Paint wand with base color of choice, using acrylic paint that dries permanent. The painting doesn't have to be that even.

10 When base coat is dry, start painting with thinned wash of black acrylic paint, making sure to get it into all the corners.

11 As you are painting, wipe off the paint with a damp kitchen wipe to leave dark paint in the cracks and corners.

12 Rub some gold paint, burnishing paste, or gold gel marker onto the raised beads to highlight them.

Use bits of wood or bark to trim your wand and use string or even cooked spaghetti instead of glue for the patterning.

wand box

A wand-box maker's craft is an exacting one. In order for it to perform its duties, the wand box must be made to precise dimensions, and none but the best boxes are capable of containing a wand's magic in its most potent state.

The wand box is typically made from enchanted cardboard between 2mm and 5mm in thickness. Tradition requires that the box is covered with a thin, but good-quality paper (or, for expensive wands, silk fabric), and that the base and lid of the wand box be covered in contrasting colors. In the example shown here, the established wandmakers have used their preferred combination of silver and black, but you may use your taste and judgment to choose any suitable colors. Specialty papers exist for covering cardboard, but any thin paper or gift wrap will do. You can even add a label to finish off your wand box in the most professional way.

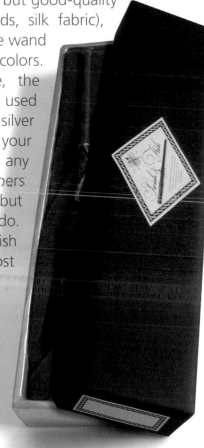

Learn the skills of a master wand-box maker to protect and display your wand in style

10 years +

60 minutes

Glue gun
Colored paper
Thick cardboard
Double sided tape
Craft knife

download available

wand box

BOX DIMENSIONS FORMULA

base	lid
Width = 7cm	Width = 7cm + (2 x CT)
Depth = 3cm	Depth = 3cm + (1 x CT)
Length = WL + 3cm	Length = WL + 3cm + (2 x CT)

WL = Wand Length CT = Cardboard Thickness

top label TEMPLATE

end label TEMPLATE

cut-away portion = half cardboard thickness

width

depth

depth

length

base and lid box net guide

Please note that this picture is drawn to scale, but it is not the correct size

wand box

Wand Length (WL)

Cardboard Thickness (CT)

1 Measure your wand length in millimeters and measure your cardboard thickness in millimeters. Using the formula on the template sheet work out the dimensions for the box base and lid.

2 The box base and lid both start out as a cross shape made from five long rectangles. The center rectangle is the shape that will need to be creased.

3 To make sure that the box folds up squarely, you will also need to remove a small bit on the side of each end tab. Remove a strip half-a-cardboard-thickness wide on each side.

4 Using a sharp craft knife, carefully cut out the base box net. Crease the cardboard deeply. If it is thick, corrugated cardboard you might have to make a V-shaped crease with the handle end of a teaspoon.

5 Put glue down each corner and fold up the sides. You can secure the box with clear sticky tape.

6 Coat your cover paper in double-sided tape, or spray glue (you can use white glue, but you will have to proceed one face at a time). Glue the box to the middle of the paper and cut four slits from the corners as shown.

▶

wand box

7 Roll the box over and glue the side on, then trim off the paper so that there is enough to fold over the box edge and about 1 cm to 1½ cm down the inside of the box.

8 Cut a slit at the corners as shown and then neatly wrap the paper over the edge and down inside the box.

9 Depending on the thickness of your cardboard, you might have to cut some little strips at the sides as shown. Cut these and tuck over and then fold around the remaining piece to partially cover the end of the box. Repeat for the other long side.

10 To finish the end, nicely fold the remaining piece over the end and down inside.

11 Using the formula from the template sheet, calculate the dimensions of the lid, then mark out and repeat instructions 3–10. Cover the top in a color that contrasts with the base.

12 When the top is covered, use a sharp craft knife to cut two semicircular cutouts in the box-lid side halfway along it.

wand box

13 Line the box with spiffy fabric. You can use felt or velvet if you have some. Cut the fabric so that it is about twice as wide and a little bit longer than the box base. Use fabric glue or glue-gun glue and working a bit at a time, run a bead of glue down the inside of the box side and glue the outside of the fabric to it. Work on one side first, and then when the glue is dry, do the same for the other side so that when you are finished, the glued part can't be seen. Just tuck the ends around and secure with a little blob of glue.

14 Trace over or download our special templates from the website and cut out the main label and two end labels. Glue them in position as shown. Fill in the blank labels with your name or the type of wand and its core. Write neatly; you are now a master wand-box builder!

A wand-box specification form and labels make the perfect finishing touches. Go to our website to print them out.

secret box book

This box looks just like a beautiful antique book and is perfect for hiding away your secrets

11 years +
2 hours
Craft knife Glue-gun glue White glue Paint (brown, black and gold) Embossed wallpaper Gold and red paper
download available

Once upon a time, not so long ago, the trade in dragons' eggs and other fire-belly related materials was banned. New laws threatened harsh punishments for anyone found in possession of prohibited contraband, but they had little effect. As is often the case, the legislation didn't really stop the sale and transport of the goods; it just pushed it underground. Collectors unwilling to give up their prized dragonolia devised ever cleverer ways of hiding their collections. One of the most favored hiding places was the hollowed book. Tucked away in a large library, secret box books (as they became known) provided an excellent and readily accessible hiding place for smallish items of high value. I have had Collinworth draw up some plans so that you can make your very own secret box book.

The plans are for one of the larger books that I believe will hold objects as broad and as tall as a sheet of office printer paper. Authentic labels, available on our website, will complete the box beautifully.

secret box book

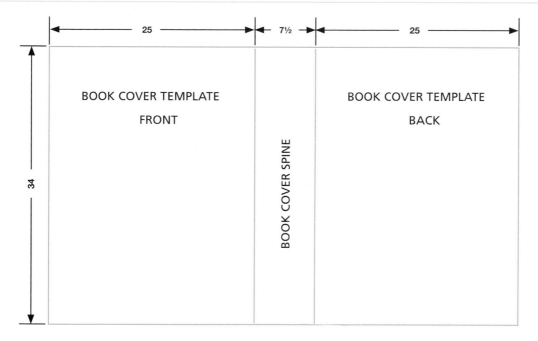

MARK OUT THESE SHAPES ON SOME THICK (5 mm) CORRUGATED CARDBOARD. IF YOUR CARDBOARD IS NOT BIG ENOUGH TO MAKE THE WHOLE BOOK COVER AND SPINE IN ONE PIECE, THEN MAKE IT FROM THREE SECTIONS AND JOIN THEM TOGETHER WITH A STRIP OF FABRIC GLUED EITHER SIDE OF THE CARDBOARD USING WHITE GLUE.

secret box book

1 Mark out and cut out the book cover using the measurements supplied on the template sheet.

2 Cut out the four crescent shapes using the templates on the label sheet on page 142.

3 Wrap the cover in a piece of embossed wallpaper. Wallpaper shops and DIY shops will always give you a small off-cut, so it will be easy to get some. Choose an organic looking pattern; I chose leaves for mine.

4 Crease or score the inside of the spine in straight lines between the spine marks that you made earlier. This will help the spine bend nicely around the crescent shapes.

5 Glue the spine round the little crescent shapes so that they are evenly spaced along the length of the spine. Make sure the two end pieces are inset from the edge of the cover so that you won't be able to see them when the book is finished.

6 Construct the box from the box sides and ends. Glue-gun glue the first side to the base and the flat fronts of the spine crescents. Then glue the other three sides on so that they are square and glued to each other and the back cover of the book.

WHITE GLUE
or
WALLPAPER
PASTE

secret box book

7 Use a pencil to mark out a rectangle on the front cover. This should be comfortably bigger than the label template.

8 Using the glue gun to create more pronounced relief, draw over the marked-out rectangle and any other features on the embossed wallpaper, like stems or flowers and so on.

9 Paint the cover dark brown using water-based, emulsion house-decorating paint or using spray paint. The paint you use must dry waterproof, otherwise it will wash off in the next step.

10 When the brown paint is dry, mix up some black acrylic paint with a little bit of water and brush on and wipe off. As the black paint stays in all the creases of the pattern, it will make the cover look old. Apply and wipe off until you get the effect you want.

11 When the black paint is dry, use gold, bronze, or silver paint or better still, rubbing paste to rub over and highlight the glue-gun strips and the most prominent parts of the embossed wallpaper pattern. Trace over the label template and design your book title, then glue it inside the rectangle.

12 Neatly cover the box/pages' with gold paper, sticking it on with white glue, or better still, double-sided sticky tape. Cover the cardboard so that the top edge is covered and the covering goes a little way down the inside of the box.

book label TEMPLATE

crescent spine formers TEMPLATE **x 4**

6cm

box edge HEIGHT

This is the height of the box sides and the maximum length of the crescent shapes.

secret box book

13 Line the inside front cover with a contrasting shade of paper and then line the inside of the box. First line the bottom of the box. Cut out a piece of lining paper with small cuts in the corners. Push the paper right down in to the corners.

14 Cut a strip of lining paper slightly smaller than the height of the box sides and line the box sides so that the bottom edge of lining paper and the side edges of gold paper are covered neatly.

15 Make a slit in the box side and push the end of a ribbon through with a blunt dinner knife; fold end over and glue on the inside of the box. Do the same at the top of the box. At the top, tuck over and glue down inside the spine for the bottom. Cut a V-shape out and seal with a dab of white glue to stop it fraying.

What will you hide inside?

feather quills

Easy to make, these real feather quills are both functional and highly magical

10 years +

1 hour

Ink jet printer
Thick printer paper
Coloring pencils or
felt-tip pens

download available

Henry stared vacantly out of the window, the nib of his quill poised an inch or so above the journal into which he had been busily scratching his version of the day's events. The feather ruffled slightly in the gentle breeze blowing through the open French doors.

"Imagine," he said, cocking his head to one side and tapping the nib on the page so that it made an ink blot, "if one could invent a quill that had everlasting ink."

Henry, my ten-year-old nephew, was staying at the summer home over the summer holidays and I had quickly come to realize that he was given to saying the strangest things. I never forgot that chance comment and decades later, as soon as the first ballpoint pens were available, I put together this little project, which neatly marries the elegance of a feather quill with the practicality and writing convenience of a ballpoint pen. I sincerely hope you enjoy it.

feather quills

1 Draw a line lengthwise down a piece of A4-sized paper about one-third of the way across the page. You can use plain paper or brightly colored gift-wrapping paper. Copy or trace the outline of the feather that you want to make from the patterns supplied or make up your own feather shape.

2 Turn the paper over and put double-sided sticky tape all over the part of the sheet where you drew the feather.

3 Take the thin cartridge out of a cheap, click-button, ballpoint pen (the writing tip must be one of the thinnest ones) and tape it to a straight piece of coathanger wire.

4 Bend the coathanger to match the gentle curve of the stem (or *rachis*, to give it its proper name). Lay it on the drawing you made and cut it to length with a pair of pliers.

5 Peel off the double-sided tape and position the pen-wire part over the stem. Note: It is much easier to see through the paper if you hold it up against a window or another light source.

6 Fold the feather over along one of its edges and then carefully press the paper down around the pen-wire part to make the stem budge out down the middle, so it looks just like a real feather.

▶

feather TEMPLATES

Hippogryph

Phoenix

Snowy Owl

feather quills

7 Paint or spray the feather on both sides. Use bright colors. Look in a picture book or search on the web to give you some ideas of the sort of beautiful markings bird feathers have. You can paint over your line, but make sure that you can still see it, so that you have something to guide you when you come to cut it out.

8 Carefully cut around the feather outline.

9 Wrap some clear tape around the bottom of the feather stem and a around the pen end to secure the pen in place and give you something to grip when you write with it.

Phoenix, Snowy Owl, and Hippogryph colored-quill designs are available to print from our website.

magical ink pot

What more useful partner to the quill could there be than a magical ink pot?

12 years +

20 minutes

A4 paper sheet
Double-sided tape
Glue gun
Hand-soap bottle cap
Single-serving drink bottle

download available

Hidden deep within the Magical Inkpot's velvety darkness are all the words of all the stories yet to be told. Take my advice, though—such rare and bewitching devices are not easy to come by. Adventurers better than I have given over large fortunes and spent many a long expedition in search of pristine examples. I am certain that the same fate would have befallen me had I not chanced up on a looseleaf portfolio within whose faded clutches lay the clear and simple instructions for a Magical Inkpot's fabrication, which I hereby pass to you.

Granted, when using the magical ink, the pen does drape itself in a certain overly rich verbosity that may on occasion get in the way of what one is actually trying to say . . . by which I mean, that is, it's easy to fall under the spell of the Magical Inkpot's delicately wrought charms . . . but there is no denying it is a great place to keep your quill.

magical ink pot

1 You will need a small drink bottle and a squeezable sauce bottle cap, with or without flip over lid.

2 Remove the rubber insert valve.

SPACE FOR LABEL

3 Mark around the bottle to cut off the top and most of the flat part of the middle, leaving some space for the label in the finished ink pot.

4 Cut the top of the bottle off. The plastic is hard here so use a hacksaw. Kids can use a junior hacksaw safely, and it's good practice, but you should steady the bottle.

5 Carefully cut the bottle to the other marks using either a craft knife or pair of strong kitchen scissors.

GLUE   GRAVEL

6 Tape the two halves of the bottle back together with sticky tape and half fill with some gravel and a bit of glue-gun glue to stop the stones rattling.

▶

GLUE

 7 Carefully glue the cap in place by gluing the underside of the cap and spray the whole thing with black spray paint.

8 Cut out some paper to fit and stick it around the base using double-sided tape or a blob of glue-gun glue.

9 All your finished ink pot needs now is a magical quill and you are ready to write your first spell.

Go to our website to print this stylish label for your ink pot.

dragon-hunter's goggles

At the height of the dragon-hunting boom, hardly a week went by without the London press running a story of some hapless adventurer, fried to a crisp in the blast of a super-heated roar. As you might imagine, a whole industry grew up selling specialized protective dragon-hunting equipment.

As a dragon hunter myself, there was one item that I would never have been without: my flare-resistant, Glaremaster goggles. Extremely lightweight with ground sapphire lenses, these wonderful goggles offer a supreme level of ocular protection for the riskiest dragon encounters.

Even now, when there are no more dragons to vanquish, the goggles come in very handy. The company that originally made my Sapphire Glaremasters over 150 years ago is no longer in business, but don't let that trouble you, because now you can make a pair yourself. Collinworth has provided you with a set of excellent instructions and a template to assist you in your efforts.

Make your own flare-resistant Glaremaster dragon-hunter's goggles

8 years +
90 minutes

Fabric or leather
2 x bottle caps
2 L soda bottle
Gold paint (pen)
Transparent, colored,
   cellophane candy
   wrapper
Glue
Velcro

dragon-hunter's goggles

1. Measure around the head. You'll be surprised how big the measurement is. Ideally, just wrap the thick fabric or preferably leather strip you are going to use around the head and mark off the length with a permanent marker. Remember to leave some overlap for the
Velcro (hook and eye) fixing.

2. Cut out the shape of the goggles from the template sheet and lay it on the fabric or leather at the center of the strip and draw around it with a marker. Then cut out the shape, including the eye holes, using a strong pair of scissors.

3. Cut most of the center from two milk bottle closures so that you leave a small rim around the edge. Some closures have a rim inside, which is useful to follow as a cutting guide. If your closures don't, then you'll need to draw a guideline around with a marker before you start cutting. Take care with sharp knives and only cut soft polythene plastic lids.

4. Paint both closures with gold paint. You can use spray, gold felt-tip markers, or gold paint. Put them on one side to dry while you make the rest of the goggles.

5. Select the circle guide that best fits the bottle lid diameter that you have. Trace the template square and then carefully cut out the correct circle.

6. Use the circle template to draw two circles on the shoulder of a 2-liter drink bottle with a permanent marker.

circle guide TEMPLATE

7 Use a craft knife to cut the bottle in half.

8 Carefully cut around the circles to make your lenses. You can get four lenses out of one 2-liter bottle.

Extend out to correct length, with overlap for hook and eye (Velcro) fixing.

goggles TEMPLATE

dragon-hunter's goggles

9 To make the inner-colored filters, cut two circles of boiled candy wrapper cellophane (or similar) about the same size as the lenses. Check out whether you can see through the sheet by holding it close to your eyes, most candy wrappers and even some chip-bag, metalized plastic foils are actually see-through if you look up close.

10 Assemble the eye pieces by first sticking the lens inside the golden ring. To do this, first put some glue inside the ring (**a**). If using glue-gun glue, wait a few seconds for it to cool slightly before pressing in the lens as the very hot glue can melt the lens slightly and spoil the look of it. Next, put a ring of glue on the goggle strap just round the eye hole (**b**) and stick the color filter film to that. Lastly, apply some glue to the underside of the ring (**c**) and stick that to the goggle strip.

11 Using a gold or silver marker or a paintbrush, make a number of small dots along the goggle strip as shown on the template. Alternatively, make up your own pattern.

12 Don't forget the Velcro (hook and eye fastener). Use a self-adhesive version and sew or stick with glue-gun glue. Remember that the Velcro is stuck to the front of one end and the back of the other end so that the strap lays flat when the Velcro is fastened.

TIP: Use a ski goggle or large glasses case to keep your Glaremasters safe and ready for use.

BIG-KITCHEN SCIENCE
Growing a crystal

This experiment involves mixing salt with water to make a saturated solution. It's a reasonably quick, fun experiment to do, but the crystal growing takes days. The experiment can be used as a basis for some interesting discussions about crystals and solutions, which you can record in a results booklet, downloadable from our website.

Cultivate a big crystal using nothing more than salt and water

When growing your salt crystal, don't use dishwasher salt as this has various anticaking additives in it that make it impossible for a big crystal to grow. Sugar also makes a fabulous crystal, but it does take much longer to form.

6 years +

1 hour (plus growing time)

Empty jam jar or drinking glass
Salt
Thread
Wire coathanger or small stick

download available

BIG-KITCHEN SCIENCE

1 Pour half a mug of salt into 600ml of warm water. Do not use salt with added anticaking agents.

SALT

2 Stir until the salt is dissolved. Keep adding a little salt and stirring until no more salt will dissolve.

3 Carefully pour the solution into a clean jam jar or glass, making sure that you don't pour any salt in.

MAGNIFIED SALT SEED CRYSTAL

4 Tie a piece of thread around the biggest salt crystal you can find in the unused salt you have.

5 Tie the thread around a piece of coathanger wire or drinking straw and dangle it in the solution.

6 Watch your salt crystal grow. But don't hold your breath; it grows slowly, very slowly.

7 Every couple of days, lift the crystal out and pour the water into another jar, leaving behind the crystals that have grown on the bottom.

8 After about a week, your crystal should have grown. Take it out and dry it carefully on kitchen paper towels, then hang it up or put it in the booklet you can download from our website.

BIG-KITCHEN SCIENCE

Experimental discussion

What is a salt crystal made of?

Trillions and trillions of sodium chloride molecules all arranged neatly in rows. As its name suggests, sodium chloride (the chemical name for salt) is made up of the two chemical elements, sodium and chlorine. The scientific way of writing this is NaCl (Na = Sodium, Cl = Chlorine). The molecules line up so that salt forms a cubic crystal.

How does the crystal grow?

As some water evaporates from the solution, the remaining water can't hold the salt in solution. The salt is deposited one molecule at a time and little crystals form. The salt molecules line themselves up in neat rows because that is the way they can fit together using the least amount of energy.

Why do we need salt?

Salt contains sodium, and sodium is a vital chemical used by the body to make nerves work and help regulate the body's water levels. However, too much is bad for us and causes high blood pressure.

How much salt is there in seawater?

There are 1½ lbs of salt for every cubic meter of seawater. However, salt only makes up about three-quarters of the minerals dissolved in seawater.

BEING THERE

Help your kids be creative

Children don't need much to fire up their imaginations, and are enthusiastic to participate in the fictional universes of their favorite game and story characters. These Great Adventures projects play to this need by adding imaginary backstories to each plan, turning the projects into voyages of discovery and providing a starting point for the richest possible interaction with each craft activity.

Children start out as naturally creative, and by helping them to develop their innate creativity you will enable them to be happier, perform better at school and be more successful as they grow up. Creativity is about so much more than drawing a pretty picture or making a great model, it is what helps your children develop the ability to see a problem from more than one angle. It helps them find new solutions by using the knowledge they already have as imaginatively as possible in a wide range of school subjects and real-life situations. Creativity will also help your children to negotiate more successfully by allowing them to see the other person's point of view. As they grow up, being creative will improve their school grades and eventually help them in their jobs and relationships.

As a parent, you are in the perfect position to develop your childrens' creativity, and it is not something that you can just leave to their teachers. Despite the fact that the modern curriculum recognizes that creativity is critical to a child's development, large classes are no match for the potential benefit of your undivided, one-on-one attention.

So, here are the first five of ten great ways to develop your child's creativity and help them fulfill their potential.

1 Fire up their imagination

Be creative when you talk to your children. Discuss with them the things you see together, whether that be television programs, films or things that happen in your neighborhood.. Tell your kids about anything interesting that you have done that day and describe the events in a way that paints a picture for them. Use descriptive words and, where appropriate, describe how you felt about the situation. Finally, take them on creative outings now and then; go to the zoo, a museum or an art gallery. It doesn't take much to get a kid's creativity and imagination going.

2 Answer their questions

Always try to answer your children's questions. Handled correctly and presented in a way that they can understand, children can take on concepts behind almost any subject, and answering their questions is a way of showing them that you approve of their inquisitiveness and respect their intelligence. Children are learning machines and are naturally very curious, so even if you don't know the answer to a question, look it up in a book or on the web.

That doesn't mean that your kids shouldn't have to think for themselves. Creativity is about batting ideas back and forth, thinking out a problem, challenging what you know and exploring the limits. If you think that they might already know the answer to their own question, then encourage them to say it. Ask them things like: "Why do you think that is?" or "What would be a better way of doing that?" or "Why do you think it works like that?" Be prepared to prompt them, but try to let them work some things out for themselves. It's quite likely that you will be surprised by how clear their thinking is and how much they really know.

3 Spend time with them to get them started

Kids need your time. They want to be with you and when they are spending time with you that they know isn't rushed, they can relax and let their creativity come to the forefront. A great way (and perhaps the most obvious way) to develop your children's creativity is to make stuff with them. It could be anything from brick models to plastic construction kits to any other type of craft. When you start out making things together, it is likely that you will have to provide most of the momentum to get things going. Persevere, let them do as much as possible, and help them out where their lack of skill is clearly frustrating them. However, try not to end up doing the whole thing yourself while they idly look on, or worse still, while they go off and play video games. If they do start to get bored, put the project away and get it out another day when they, and you, are fresh. From a creative point of view, the process is just as important as the end result.

Don't be put off if what you make together doesn't come out as hoped. If you keep trying, the end results will get better and better as you and your child practice and improve.

4 Provide them with the kit

It's always said that a poor workman blames his tools, but there is nothing more frustrating than trying to do something with the wrong equipment. Depending on what you plan to do, make sure that you have a small crafting kit ready. Whether you are going to make something from this book or just invent something, then a few permanent marker felt pens, some quick-dry glue or a glue gun and a couple of cans of spray paint are all you'll really need for most projects.

Creativity doesn't have to be limited to doing specific 'creative' projects. When you go out, if you are going to be in the car or on the train, take a pad and one or two pencils with you. A kit like this not only makes any journey much easier but also can provide a nice extra dimension to the day out itself when you stop to draw one of the animals at the zoo, or something you've seen in the park.

5 Provide them with the opportunity

Sometimes you might have to turn off the television and the computer console and get all the crafting materials out to get your kids started. You could:

- Have a painting and doing afternoon. On a sunny afternoon, get a roll of blank lining wallpaper, unroll as much as possible on your garden fence and let the kids paint it with washable poster paints, making as much mess as they like
- Play creative games like Pictionary or card games where there is an element of negotiation and decision making, Go Fish, for example
- Learn how to play classic card games like 21s, Gin Rummy or Spades

All these games and types of activity require creativity and original ways of problem-solving, and although some of the games can take time to learn they are very satisfying to play well.

secret box book PAGE 138

*My father gave me
the greatest gift
anyone could give
another person, he
believed in me.*

JAMES (JIMMY V) VALVANO
Basketball coach

ray gun PAGE 169

space rocket

Make a rocket ship from old packaging you have lying around

8 years +	
1 hour	

Glue gun
Marker
Craft knife
Chip tube
Single-serving drink bottle
Yogurt carton
Toilet paper roll
Shaving-foam cap
Cardboard
Paper

You don't have to be a rocket scientist to make a rocket from junk packaging. These instructions show you how to do it with a chip tube and a toilet paper tube, but any collection of tubes will do. Cut off a single-serving drink bottle top for the engine nozzle and a deodorant spray cap for the nose cone and the rest is easy.

For our rocket, I didn't stick the chip tube lid down—that meant we could take it apart and later we made a simple satellite to go inside so that when "in space" the satellite could be deployed.

Here are some tips:
1. Cover the tubes in white A4 paper before you glue them together so that you can draw on them easily; this saves you from having to paint them.

2. Draw your graphics and some black lines and boxes onto the paper before you wrap it around the tubes; it's much easier to draw on flat paper!

1 Cover the chip tube and the toilet roll tube in white paper.

2 Cut the top and bottom off a single- serving drink bottle. Glue the yogurt cup upside down on top of the chip tube, glue the toilet roll tube on the bottom of the yogurt cup, cap this with the bottom of the single-serving bottle, and glue the shaving-foam cap on the top as the nose cone.

3 Glue the top of the drink bottle on the bottom of the chip tube as the engine cone.

4 Fold four pieces of thick cardboard in half and draw on the shape of the leg with a marker, making sure that the side and bottom are at right angles. Cut through both thicknesses with strong scissors or a knife. Mark straight lines on a shower gel bottle, then cut off the shoulders to use as engine bulges.

DECORATE

CRUMPLED
WRAPPING
PAPER

5 Glue legs and engine bulges in position, making sure the rocket stands straight. Stick on small pieces of discarded building bricks for detail. Stick crumpled wrapping paper or tin foil around engine cone and decorate with a marker pen. It's as simple as that. . . .Blast off!

Give your rocket a name for its first launch. Kids love naming things that they have made. It adds the finishing touches and gives them a real sense of pride.

spaceship

This is such an easy and pleasing project and has given my children hours of fun. As the cleaning-liquid bottle (the canopy part) was made of clear plastic, we sprayed the inside of that black before sticking it to the body to make it look really shiny when finished. Just remember to mask off the window part before spraying the rest of the body color. Once the red—or any other body color you like—has been sprayed, you can use artists' acrylic paints to finish it off. Use a wash of black to make certain parts look old, worn-out, or dirty, and paint contrasting colors as lines and rings in certain places to add detail. You can also add alien-looking numbers or letters.

Trace over the special wing template provided. For our wings we used foamboard, but any thick or corrugated cardboard would be just as good for the job.

Make this incredible spaceship and look like a professional model maker

12 years +
1 hour (including glue drying)

Craft knife
Glue gun
Marker
Hacksaw
Shower gel bottle
Liquid hand-soap bottle
2 x Toothbrushes
2 x Felt-tip pens
Cardboard

spaceship

 1 Trace over the wing template, stick it on to some thick cardboard, and carefully cut it out using a craft knife. **Take care with sharp knives; do not let children use them without help. Use strong scissors where possible.**

2 Offer the cut-out wing up to the side of the shower gel bottle and mark off a slot for the wing tab. (Use the seam of the bottle as a guide.) Cut out the hole with a craft knife.

 3 Use glue-gun glue or very rapid epoxy resin to glue the wings to the shower gel bottle, pushing the wing tab fully into the slot you cut in the side of the bottle. **Note: the wings are swept forward.**

4 Using a hacksaw or serrated knife, cut the two, old felt-tip pens down in size so that they just fit over the wings.

Also cut the handle ends off two old toothbrushes.

5 Glue the caps on the felt pens and then stick the cut-off felt pens against the fuselage on the top of each wing.

 6 Stick the wing thickener on top of the wing, pushed up against the felt pen barrel.

spaceship

7 Using glue-gun glue, attach the cut-off toothbrush handles on to the wing tips.

8 To make the cockpit canopy, use a permanent marker to draw diagonally across the corner of a thin bottle and then carefully cut out the shape using a craft knife or strong scissors.

wing **TEMPLATE**

spaceship

9 Offer the canopy to the fuselage (but do **not** glue it yet) and marker around it.

10 Glue-gun glue is too hot for the thin bottle when it comes out of the gun, so put glue onto the fuselage and wait 10–15 seconds before pushing the canopy into place.

11 Push canopy down onto glue ring.

12 Paint the spaceship according to your own color scheme.

TIP: If you use corrugated cardboard, you could seal up the edge of the wing with glue-gun glue to give a better finish.

ray gun

My sons thought up some inventive equipment inspired by the games they like best—handheld arms that shoot whirlwinds, suck up water, or even turn things into chickens. Having looked at what junk we had in the 'making box', we decided to make this ray gun, called a *pulse rifle*, which shoots out a laser ray with rings of light surrounding it.

It's not that hard to put together, but the skill is in making it so that it looks like a pulse rifle, and if you get the grip size right, it feels great in the hand. Once we had finished making it, the kids even abandoned the virtual game for awhile in favor of acting out the story themselves.

Get your kids up out of their chairs

| 10 years + |
| 90 minutes |

Detergent bottle
Sport drink bottle
Single-serving drink
   bottle
Pieces of aluminium
   foil
Glue gun
Drinking cup
Thick cardboard
Spray paint

ray gun

1 To make the stock, either use a thin, wide, short bottle or make your own by cutting down a thin washing-detergent bottle as shown. Carefully mark around the bottle horizontally and then cut the bottle with a pair of strong scissors. Check the size of the bottle where you mark so that one end fits neatly inside the other.

GLUE

A

2 For the best effect, use glue-gun glue and apply to the rim that fits inside the other and then push the two parts of the bottle together, making sure that they are straight.

B

3 Mark and then cut about two-thirds off a plastic disposable cup to make the muzzle end.

4 The barrel is made in two parts. A straight metallic part and a larger-shaped part. The straight part is simply made by wrapping a piece of tin foil around a toilet paper tube. Thicker foil is better, so used takeaway food trays are ideal, but any kitchen foil will do. The second, shaped part of the barrel is made from an old sports drink bottle (see assembly, step 13).

C

5 The telescopic sight makes this model really fun to play with. The sight is made from any small single-serving drink bottle. Glue thin strips of foil in the shape of a cross over the open neck of the bottle.

ray gun

6 Cut a hole in the base of the bottle and glue-gun glue a lid from a cleaning-detergent bottle over it. The live-hinged cap lid is now the sight scope cover. If you put your eye up to the small hole, you can see the cross hairs clearly at the other end. Cut a small parallelogram-shaped piece of thick cardboard for the site mount and glue it to the side of the bottle.

8 Wrap the grip block in paper, lightweight cardboard, or thick aluminium foil. Trim off the wrapping to the edge of the thick cardboard block.

7 Make the grip using the template provided. Mark out and cut four long, thin, identically sized, parallelogram-shaped pieces of thick cardboard and glue them together to make a single block.

9 Although glue-gun glue is strong, the top of the grip will see a lot of stress during play, so cut two strengthening plates from thick cardboard. To make sure that they will fit the shape of the stock, draw around its profile with a marker.

grip TEMPLATE

ray gun

10 Glue the support plates either side of the grip so that the top of the plates line up with the cut top of the grip block.

11 Cut out a square of thick cardboard slightly bigger than the end of the grip and glue to the end of the grip.

12 For a neat finish, paint each part before assembling the ray gun. Choose whatever colors you like. Ray guns always seem to be brightly colored, especially in your favorite video games.

13 Assemble the parts as shown.

14 Decorate the ray gun with electrical tape, and glue drinking straws (sprayed silver) between the stock and the expansion barrel. Add extra finishing touches using whatever you have at hand: wires, springs, or little bits of circuit board. In fact, anything vaguely technical-looking will add great detail.

E

B

ELECTRICAL TAPE

D

C

A

DRINKING STRAWS

E

Now how cool is that? And it was all made from junk packaging saved up over a couple of weeks.

satellite

For thousands of years, humans have gazed up into the velvety blanket of the night sky in wonder. In 1995, the Hubble Space Telescope stared deep into space for ten days and built up an image of what it could see stretching right to the edge of the visible universe. The image it showed us is mind-blowing. In an area of sky that is only the size of the eye of a needle held at arm's length, the Hubble imaged at least 1,500 galaxies. Given that each galaxy has around 500 billion stars in it, in just that one tiny portion of the night sky, the Hubble was looking at a mind-boggling 750 trillion stars. Now with that thought running through your head, go and make a model of the Hubble Space Telescope to remind yourself how amazing the universe really is.

Make your own model satellite, just like the Hubble Space Telescope

10 years +

90 minutes

2 x Toilet paper
  tubes
Kitchen foil
Paper clips
Sieve mesh
Craft knife
Glue-gun glue
Marker
Gold paint
Cardboard

satellite

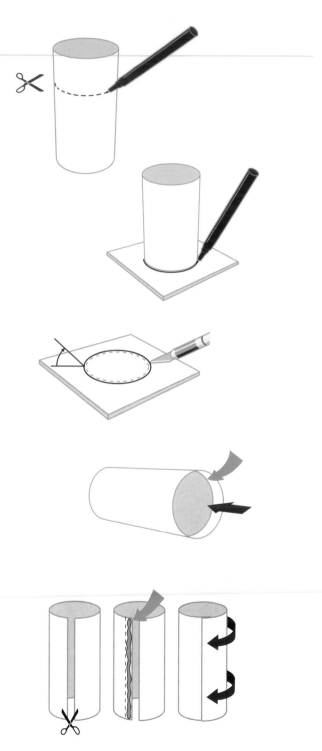

1 Mark a horizontal line about two-thirds of the way along a toilet paper tube and then neatly cut around the line.

2 Carefully mark around the tube (making sure that you don't squeeze it into an oval shape) to make a circle the same size as the tube on a thick piece of corrugated cardboard or foamboard.

3 Carefully cut out the circle just inside the line. If you make the cut at a slight angle, it will really help you in the next stage, when you have to fit the cardboard circle inside the toilet paper tube end.

4 The base is recessed. Check that the circle fits before you add the glue. If it is too big, mark where it doesn't fit and trim it to fit. For a neat finish, when gluing, put the glue inside the end of the tube and push the cardboard circle into the tube. This keeps the outside of the tube neat and free of glue, and the circle wipes the glue down inside the tube. Put this to one side and now make the second tube.

5 The satellite telescope is made of two concentric tubes (much like an old- fashioned, handheld ship's telescope), so the second tube needs to fit inside the first one. The thinner tube is longer than the one you have just prepared, so it doesn't need to be cut shorter. Instead, make a vertical cut in the second tube and glue it back together so that the cut edges overlap and it has a smaller diameter.

6 Check that the new, thinner tube fits inside the first one you made. It does not have to be a tight fit. Cover both tubes in slightly crumpled aluminium kitchen foil. This is easily done by rolling the foil around the tubes and then tucking the ends over. Stick it to the tubes using glue-gun glue or double-sided sticky tape for a quick result.

9 Spray the entire assembly with gold paint. If you don't have gold paint, use white or leave the original silver of the aluminium foil. Spray the lid end first; as the lid is made of cardboard, it will dry quickly. As soon as the lid is dry, you can hold the assembly by the edge of the lid and spray the rest without ending up with gold fingers.

7 To make the telescope lid, cut a small, table-tennis-bat-shaped piece of thin corrugated cardboard, so that the circle is about the same diameter as that of the thinner of the two tubes.

10 To make the solar cells, cut out two rectangles of thin corrugated cardboard about as wide as the tube and nearly as long as the telescope. Stick two slightly smaller rectangles of holographic wrapping paper (or similar) onto the panels (one on each side). Bend a paper clip at right angles and glue into the thickness of the cardboard. Use paper clips to make other surface details or to break up the panel into smaller subpanels.

8 Glue the thinner tube inside the thicker one. For a neat result, put the glue inside the thicker tube and push the thinner tube onto the glue. You only need to push the thinner tube about 1cm in. Make sure that the foil seams line up. Glue the telescope lid into the inside of the open end of the thinner tube with its handle on the opposite side to the seams.

▶

To make the satellite communications dish, carefully straighten and then bend a large paper clip as shown.

Mark around the shape on a piece of thick cardboard.

Carefully cut a hole out of the cardboard, at a slight angle if possible. You are going to be using this as the former for a small bit of mesh, so an angled cut will help you get a satellite dish-shaped mesh.

To make the satellite dish, ideally you should use a soft metal mesh of the type used in auto-body repair. It can be bought at most car shops in small sheets. It is low cost and cuts and forms easily. If you can't get hold of that, use a small piece of aluminium foil.

Apply a ring of glue-gun glue to the round part of the satellite frame and glue the mesh onto it so that the ring of the frame lines up with the indent you have made in the mesh.

17 The solar panels and the satellite dish are attached to the main telescope assembly at the joint between the two tubes. Choose where you want to attach them and put a small blob of glue-gun glue at the joint, then push the paper clip in between the two tubes and hold until the glue sets.

18 Make other aerials and more satellite dishes if you want and attach them in the same way.

16 When the glue is set, carefully cut around the frame, cutting away the excess mesh. Make a right-angled bend in the end of the paper clip.

The real Hubble Space Telescope is the size of a small truck and weighs over 11 tons.

Make a hydrometer

Test the density of liquids with this simple-to-make hydrometer

The world is an interesting place, and you are one of the best people to show your children just how fascinating it is. On page 180, there are a few key facts about the experiment designed to help you engage your children's interest and explain in simple terms what's going on in the experiment.

6 years +

20 minutes

Cheap ballpoint pen
Drinking glass
Blu-Tack
Glue gun (optional)

download available

This experiment involves mixing water with salt or sugar and seeing the difference it makes to the thickness (mass or specific gravity) of water by measuring it with a homemade hydrometer. Once made, the hydrometer can be used to measure the relative specific gravity of a range of water-based fluids and drinks. The experiment can be used as a basis for some interesting discussions about solvents and solutes and how things dissolve and will reinforce subjects your kids will be learning at school at some point. Go to our website to print a neat little fold-up book that can be filled in and is something nice to keep as a record of the experiment you did together.

1 Take one cheap ballpoint pen.

2 Remove the nib and ink reservoir.

3 Plug one end with a little glue-gun glue.

4 Push a blob of Sticky Tack on the same end.

5 Fill a large glass with water and slowly lower the hydrometer into the water.

6 Adjust the weight of the hydrometer by adding or removing some Sticky Tack until it floats as low as possible in the water

7 Carefully mark the water level on the hydrometer with a permanent marker.

 8 Mix up some different solutions (i.e., using salt or sugar) and float the hydrometer in each of them and mark each to see the difference.

Experimental discussion

? Why does the hydrometer float, given that it is open at the top?

The fluid it displaces weighs less for the same volume (has less mass) than the hydrometer.

? Why does the sugar and/ or salt (solute) dissolve in the water (solvent)?

The sugar or salt molecules are broken off by the water and mingle with the water molecules. **Note:** This is a physical reaction and is therefore reversible. You can make it go back so that you have sugar and water separated again.

? Why does the hydrometer float at different levels in the different solutions?

The solutions are denser than water, thus weigh more per volume (mass), and so the mass of the hydrometer displaces less of their volume and as a result floats higher.

? How is a hydrometer used in the real world?

Manufacturers of beer use a hydrometer to check how much alcohol is dissolved in their beers.

BEING THERE

Help your kids be creative—part two

6

Plan your creative time

When you start out on a making project, have a clear idea of what you want to make and roughly how you are going to make it. Whether you follow an existing plan or make one of your own, preparation is an essential part of doing any project. Usually kids (and most likely you) will want to dive straight in and start sticking things together, but while this is great instant fun, it is not developing your creativity. Talking through the best ways of putting items together, which paint colors to use, and what order to do things in will give your kids invaluable problem-solving experience.

At school, your children will have been taught that the most important part of any project is the plan, but often they see this as the boring part of the project where nothing is getting done. However, if you can make the planning quick and fun, it is potentially one of the most inventive times, the moment when all things are possible and you can fantasize about how fabulous the finished thing will be.

Why not:

- Get your children to look for junk packaging and any materials and equipment you are going to need
- With your kids, draw some quick sketches of the finished item, showing which parts go where
- Discuss any problems that you think you might encounter and work out how you are going to solve them. This may involve trying out to see how things go together before you stick them together permanently.

7

Do creative things that the children like

Although one aspect of creativity is complete freedom of expression, by far the most useful application of creativity is to solve problems and make things the way you want them. Creative activities with your children will be much more fun if they relate to something that the kids really like already and for which they need something that you can make together. You could design and make:

- A trading-card display book
- A football team score chart
- A prop from a recent movie
- An artifact from one of their video games

Kids love to make their games real by role-playing their way through stories and scenes that they have seen on television, at the movies, or on their video games. They will be amazed to find out that with your help they can make items and props from their favorite stories that will allow them to translate the game into their real-life, role-play versions. Things you make together are likely to be much more fun and more played with than store bought merchandise, as well as being a whole lot cheaper, as well as helping you understand what movies they like and what exactly is going on in their favorite video game.

helicopter PAGE 105

8 Don't rush them

While there should be an emphasis on completing tasks, doing something creatively is not a race. Children participate in so many activities that are geared towards winning that it is hard for them to understand that getting something done and solving problems, so that the end result is what they want, is better than finishing first.

In our society, we are obsessed with the need to instill a desire to win in our children. In most cases, this only results in turning out grown-ups who at some level are disappointed with themselves and their lives because it is impossible for everyone to win or for even the most talented person to win all the time. Developing creativity is not in itself about winning. In the long run, approaching life creatively will make you more successful and happier. When doing projects with your children, don't make them rush to false deadlines. You can always put the stuff away and get it out next time, or if they want, finish it for them so they can play with it when it's finished.

9 Don't use false praise

When you are pleased that your children are doing something creative and you want to encourage them, it is very hard not to tell them how brilliant what they are doing is—even when it is clearly not. Children are very perceptive to emotions and know when someone is saying something that they don't really mean. On the other hand, children need to feel that you approve of them and that you are proud of them. As a parent, it's very difficult to judge how good something that your child has done really is, because you have very little to compare it with. If you do a lot of crafting with your children, you get to know when they are doing something that is very good and something of which they are proud, and then you can tell them that

it is amazing. As you work together with your children, you will also develop a way of discussing the things that you do that is not judgmental, where you can assess the quality of the outcome together.

However, to start with, consider what they are doing in terms of their age and the amount of experience or practice they have had at it. If things don't turn out exactly as planned and could do with improvement, use comments like, "That's great for a first try" or "I think that that is very good for someone your age" or "That color you have chosen is perfect for that model," all of which are much better than any false flattery. Ask your children which bit of the project they liked doing the most and which bit they didn't like doing. Ask them how they could improve it if they had another go at it. During the project, if you see things going wrong, helping them with what's causing a problem will go a long way towards improving the final outcome. Don't wrestle the tools or project from them though, or they will feel that it has started to become your project and not theirs. Offer to help. Ask them: "What can I do to help?", "Do you need me to hold something?", "Do you need some help spraying because the button is too hard to press?" Remember, the act of making something is at least as important as the finished article.

Don't be negative about their ideas 10

Developing your children's creativity is about showing them how to have more ideas and giving them the skills to choose the best ones to improve the outcome. There are a few classic techniques for generating and developing ideas and lines of thinking. None of them rely on negative comments.

Negative comments stifle creativity. They inhibit the free flow of ideas from one person to another because being in an atmosphere of negative comments makes most people think twice about putting their ideas forward. When this happens, vital ideas are lost and only the most insensitive individuals or those with the loudest voices get heard. To develop your children's creativity, listen to their ideas. If you feel that they are stuck in a rut thinking about a solution that is not right, then help them build on it and develop it, and encourage them to think about the problem from an alternative viewpoint.

If you would like to make more of the idea-generating process, then you might like to try the classic ideation technique of writing the ideas on sticky notes and putting them on a wall. Use a big marker to write with so that only the core nugget of each idea can be captured. Write one idea per sticky note and try to break down the ideas into their most basic elements. These might be multiple answers to such

questions as: "What would be the best glue to use?" or "What should we use for the main body of the model?" or "Does it need to float?" As the ideas start to flow, the sticky notes can be moved about, enabling you to group the ideas together with other similar ideas into themes. By doing this, you can see if there are areas that you have missed. When you do this with your kids, remember to keep your role as facilitator, adding ideas only to spark new areas to consider and encouraging your children to consider the problem thoroughly.

fluffy ladybug PAGE 35

A father is someone that
holds your hand at the fair
makes sure you do what your mother says
holds back your hair when you are sick
brushes that hair when it is tangled
because mother is too busy
lets you eat ice cream for breakfast
but only when mother is away
he walks you down the aisle
and tells you everything's gonna be ok.

UNKNOWN

wizard's cake box PAGE 190

fold-up paper shirts PAGE 203

fluffy birthday cake PAGE 200

love heart gift box

Give a present to someone you love in this gorgeous handmade heart-shaped box

8 years +

2 hours (plus drying)

Cardboard
Newspaper
White glue
Paint

This lovely little project will show you how to make a papier-mâché box, just like the ones that you can buy in the store. Getting the lid to fit is a piece of cake, and the end result is the perfect way to wrap even the most expensive present.

We've painted ours on the outside with bright-red acrylic paint; it covers the papier-mâché perfectly and can then be easily varnished with paint or spray to give a glossy finish. Paint the inside with a contrasting color for a really nice effect. Fill the little box with pink tissue, torn and crumpled paper shreds, or like we have, with teased-out cotton wool balls. That way, whatever present you put inside will be kept safe, as well as looking beautiful when the box is opened. Choose one of the different-sized, love-heart templates and trace over it to make your box.

1 Trace over the template page and stick it to a piece of thick cardboard; select the size of heart you want and cut out. Draw around the cutout onto another piece of cardboard and cut out a second heart exactly the same size. Make sure your cuts are vertical.

2 Trace the template; measure and use it to cut two strips of cardboard for as wide as the depth of the box you want and glue vertically around one-half of one of the heart shapes (glue-gun glue is the best and quickest way to do this). Prebending the cardboard by pulling it over the edge of a tabletop helps get the curve right.

3 Glue the second heart shape to the top edge of the thin cardboard so that the two heart shapes are parallel and square to the thin cardboard, upright section.

4 Glue the second strip of cardboard around the double heart shape, making sure that it lines up and does not overhang the edge. When set, carefully trim off any excess cardboard that overhangs.

5 Pencil mark a line around the box so that the box is divided one-third/two-thirds and then, using a sharp craft knife, cut the box through all the way around at the line.

6 Tear small strips of newspaper and using white glue, cover the whole of both halves of the box (top and base) so that no part of the cardboard is visible.

▶

love heart gift box

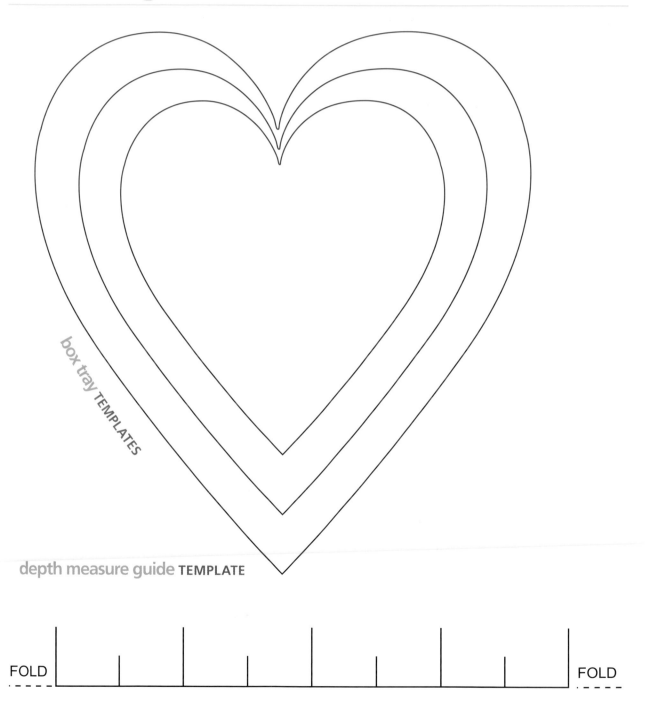

box tray TEMPLATES

depth measure guide TEMPLATE

FOLD

FOLD

x 2

7 Cut two strips of thin cardboard about ½ cm to 1 cm wider than the depth of the box bottom tray.

8 Glue into the bottom tray so that the cardboard pokes up above the edge of the tray by less than the depth of the top tray, inside depth.

9 Paint the lid and base bright red; paint designs on the box; and/or paint the inside a contrasting color. Gloss varnish the outside and fill with cotton wool and your gift.

This gift box makes the perfect Valentine's Day present—either on its own or filled with something beautiful.

wizard's cake box

Create your own special box for cakes and sweets

12 years +

10 minutes

A4 paper
Stapler (optional)

download available

It was the success of Honeydukes, Hogsmeade's most famous sweet shop, which led three brothers to set up their own magical treat and cake shops. They baked and made all manner of delicious things and came to be known for their excellence throughout the wizarding world. Each shop had its own distinctive box, but being brothers, they followed each other's designs.

Now, for the first time, you can make these boxes simply and quickly from a single sheet of A4 thick paper or light cardboard. Follow the template and cut the box out as accurately as you can, paying particular attention to the folding, because it is that which gives the box its neat appearance and shape. Gorgeous, cake box graphic printables are available on our website.

Use these boxes to pack and keep your small cakes, sweets, and treats just like a wizard, or give them as a lovely gift to that special person.

wizard's cake box

1. Trace the box template onto thin cardboard or print out the downloadable designs from our website. Carefully cut it out with a pair of scissors or use a scalpel and ruler for a very neat finish.

2. If you are using the printable from our website, place it printed face down and fold in all the side folds to the lines marked on the printed side.

3. Open out the folds and fold the sheet the other way to the lines marked.

4. Fold flat again and then begin to fold up properly; fold up so that you can fold the sides in so that they line up with each other.

5. Fold the outside edges of the box over the sides.

6. Secure the sides of the box with one staple in the middle of each side. Put the foot of the stapler inside the box so that the smooth part of the staple is showing on the outside (it looks neater).

▶

cake box TEMPLATE

wizard's cake box

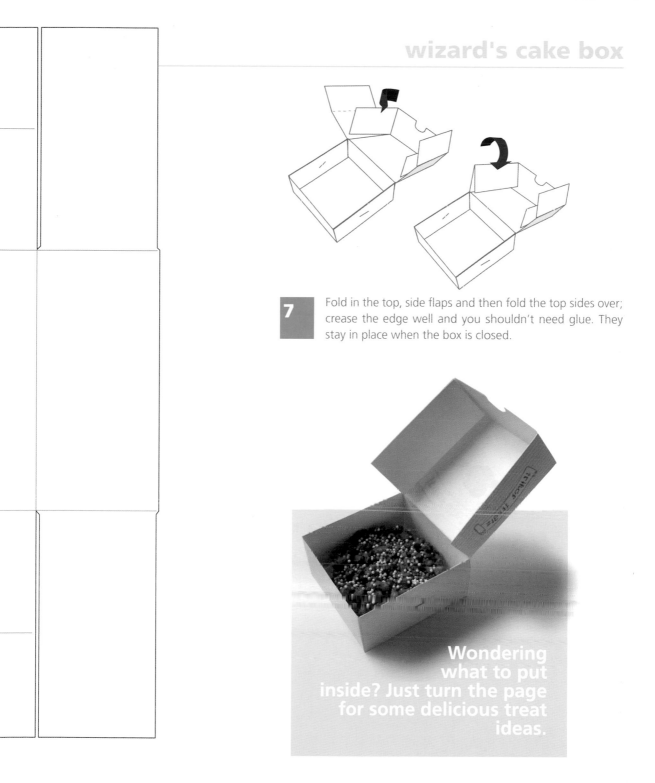

7 Fold in the top, side flaps and then fold the top sides over; crease the edge well and you shouldn't need glue. They stay in place when the box is closed.

Wondering what to put inside? Just turn the page for some delicious treat ideas.

sugar mice

Make these cute little sugar mice and then gobble them all up!

7 years +

40 minutes

2 x Mixing bowls or jugs
500g Icing
1 Egg (medium)
Lemon juice
10ml Peppermint essence (optional)
10 ml Water
Sugar laces

Sugar mice are wonderfully easy to make. No cooking is required, and provided you are careful with the amount of water or liquid you add (you only need a tiny amount), you should have very little trouble making some lovely little mice at your first attempt. For this recipe, I have used sugar laces for the tails and added some ready-mixed, chocolate-fudge-detail icing. This is great for kids to use; it comes in handy little tubes in a range of colors and is really fun to apply as the finishing touch. Don't worry if your kids' mice are all misshapen and have odd eyes. The fun is in the making and then later——the eating. You don't need to add the lemon juice or traditional peppermint essence, so all you really need is some icing and an egg and you're off and running.

sugar mice

1 Separate an egg so that you have only the white of one egg in a mixing bowl. To do this, you crack and open the eggshell and tip the yolk back and forth between the two halves of the shell, letting the white dribble out.

2 Lightly whisk up the egg white so that it is a little bit frothy. If you have it, add a few drops of lemon juice, or if you want your mice to have a peppermint taste, then add a couple of drops of peppermint essence, although neither of these are necessary.

3 Pour three-quarters of the contents of a packet of icing sugar into another mixing bowl. You will probably be able to make about ten mice with this. It's a good idea to save some icing sugar so that you have some to add to the mixture later if it gets too wet.

4 I can't stress how little water you need to add to the icing sugar in order to make the icing dough. Add the egg white; mix a drop at a time, and mix it into the icing sugar. You are aiming for a thick, solid but pliable dough. If your egg white mixture isn't enough you can add a few drops of water at the end.

5 When the icing dough is solid and pliable, take it out of the bowl and roll it on a clean, dry surface that you have lightly dusted with icing sugar. The dough should be firm enough to keep its shape if you roll it into a big ball. If it is still a bit runny, put it back in the bowl and add some more icing sugar.

ICING SUGAR

EGG WHITE

WATER

▶

sugar mice

6 When you have got the dough to a firm, stable consistency, pinch off a small amount about the size of a large marble and roll it into a ball between the palms of your hands. Make sure your hands are clean and dry.

7 Make simple, smooth mouse shapes from each ball by gently pinching the sides of one end to make the nose. An ideal shape is a teardrop that has been flattened on the base. Do not make your mice too big, because they will take a long time to set, and it is likely that they will slump as they set. Plus, it will be too much to eat at one time!

8 The tails are made from confectionary sugar laces. Make a hole in the back of the mouse using a cocktail stick or a thin chopstick and poke the sugar lace in as far as possible, carefully smoothing the hole around the lace once it is poked right in.

9 The eyes are the finishing touch. To make them, first make one hole in each side of the head end with a cocktail stick, then either drop a tiny bead of melted chocolate into the hole or use store-bought, pre-prepared chocolate fudge icing dispensed conveniently from a small tube.

Eeny, meeny, miny, moe ...

origami money box

The word origami comes from a combination of the Japanese words *oru* meaning folding and *gami* meaning paper. Traditionally, origami requires the starting paper to be cut into a perfect square, but this creation uses rectangular paper—so, what better starting point for an origami model than the original folding stuff—money?

The simple folds needed to make this lovely little open box can be learned in a few minutes. Crisp, new dollar bills make beautifully detailed boxes, and as there is no tearing involved, the money can be easily unfolded and spent; double the fun. If you're giving money as a gift, why not make it more inventive by using two different-sized banknotes to form a closing box, with one box fitting inside the other, then very carefully wrap it up neat

Transform a dollar bill with this great party trick

7 years +
5 minutes
Rectangular piece of paper or dollar bills

origami money box

1 Take one small, rectangular piece of paper, such as a dollar bill, bus ticket, or receipt.

2 Fold in half lengthwise.

3 Unfold and lay flat.

4 Fold two-thirds of one side over.

5 Fold that half back so that one side is concertina folded as far as the center line.

6 Repeat for the other side, so that the concertina folds meet neatly in the middle.

7 Fold the top layer of one side over to the other side.

8 Fold each of the corners in of the top layer. On one side, this is a single sheet; on the other, it is a double sheet.

9 Fold back the single layer.

10 Now you have to repeat the whole process for the other side. Fold over the top layer.

11 Turn the corners over so they neatly meet in the middle.

13 Pull apart the box so that it opens up.

12 Fold back the single layer so that you have a hexagonal piece of paper.

14 Shape the box at the corners by pinching the paper into nice, neat creases.

A brilliant way to leave a tip in a restaurant!

fluffy birthday cake

This cute little cake makes an original birthday present

6 years +

1 hour

Cream wool
Red wool
Paper
String
Party candle holder

download available

What could be more creative and fun than a pompom in the shape of a birthday cake? This is great for your kids to make as a gift, and if you're brave enough, it also makes a fantastic party game.

Two colors of wool are needed for the birthday cake pompom, although you could always make the jam filling using felt or material, or spray paint onto the wool through a mask. Either way, you just need to choose two suitable colors. If you are feeling really inspired, why not try icing the cake with glue-gun glue for a surreal look? Use the least amount of jam-colored wool possible, as otherwise your jam layer will be too thick. As with the spooky flowers and fluffy ladybug projects, this pompom can be made with plastic bags instead of wool, so you can get going on this cake right away!

fluffy birthday cake

1. Trace the pompom disc template on page 40 onto a thin piece of cardboard and cut out two discs.

2. Prepare the wool by doubling it up so that you have pieces about 6.5ft long in bundles of about six to ten strands, depending on how thick the wool is. You may need three or four such bundles.

3. Pass the wool through the hole in the middle of the disc repeatedly so that you wind it around the disc. Start with a red bundle, making sure that the red wool thinly covers the entire disc. This is the jam layer, and you don't want it too thick.

4. When the red bundle has covered the disc, cut the waste off and start with the cake-colored bundle. Pass that through the disc hole repeatedly until you can't pass any more wool through the hole in the middle.

5. Using strong scissors, push one blade of the scissors into the wool and between the two cardboard discs and cut the wool around the rim. You will need to help the children with this as poking the scissors in can be tricky.

6. Pass several short strands of the wool between the discs, tie them tightly around the bundle, and cut off below the ends of the pompom.

7. Remove the cardboard discs and trim the top, bottom, and sides of the pompom to make it flatter and more cake shaped.

x2

8 X 6.5ft

▶

fluffy birthday cake

8 To make the candle, tightly roll up a small piece of colored paper and glue. Then add the flame using pieces of yellow wool or felt. You can even add wax dribbles down the side of the candle using glue-gun glue.

11 Using strong scissors, cut the top into a neat curve and then cut a number of small semicircles out of the triangle so that the center of each is at the folded edge.

9 To make the doily, fold a square piece of paper over once into half and then into quarters...

12 Unfold your doily and smooth out (or iron). Glue the candle directly into the cake or use a real birthday candle holder. Glue the candle in the holder and glue the holder into the cake.

10 . . . then fold in half twice more so that you have a long, thin triangle.

Get ready to make a wish...

fold-up paper shirts

So you want to be a tailor and make some of the most beautifully pressed shirts in town? Well, this is the Japanese art of paper folding (*origami*)—with a new twist. This paper craft couldn't be simpler, and you don't need to buy any special paper. The easy-to-follow instructions show you how to fold up a shirt from a rectangular piece of office printer paper, ready for you to design and decorate however you choose. You'll also find lots of eye-catching designs for you to print and use on our website. These shirts make brilliantly original greetings cards, and they are guaranteed to make a great impression and show someone that you really care. Learn the folds, and then next time you're bored at work or school, make a paper shirt from that fax from accounts, or the note from your teacher...

Let your imagination run wild with these fold-up paper shirts

7 years +

5 minutes

Sheet of A4 paper

download available

fold-up paper shirts

1 Place paper on a flat surface.

2 Carefully fold in half lengthways and then unfold.

3 Fold the outside edges into the center line, taking care to make accurate folds.

4 Fold the bottom corners out to the edges.

5 Fold the whole bottom edge over, level with the folds you have just made.

6 Unfold bottom edge you have just folded over.

7 Unfold the corners and turn them in on themselves so that they are tucked under and your piece looks like this.

8 Pull the inside of the folded-in corners.

9 Press down so that corner folds along the outside edge of the piece.

A.

B.

C.

10 Press down and crease edge to make a neat triangle pointing at right angles to the edge.

11 Your piece should look like picture **A**. Now turn it over.

12 Fold the other edge over. Your piece should look like picture **B**. Now turn back over.

13 Fold top edges over so that the collar corners meet in the middle.

14 Fold the bottom of the piece up to the top so that it tucks under the collar folds and press down the bottom crease to make it permanent.

15 Your finished shirt should look like picture **C**. Get designing! You can also visit our website to print out lots of exciting shirt designs.

Why not try out one of your designs on the real thing? Paint the T-shirt on page 75.

handmade envelopes

Make yours a letter to remember

6 years +	
5 minutes	
Rectangular piece of paper	
download available	

Getting a letter in the mail from a friend or someone you care about is one of life's great pleasures. Now you can make someone's day by creating your own lovely envelopes and sending one yourself.

These envelopes are really quick to make and by decorating a plain white or colored piece of paper, you can turn your letter into a real piece of art. On our website, you'll find a range of patterns to print out and use, and the envelope is designed so that the pattern is on the inside, making these envelopes beautifully subtle. Whether it's Get Well Soon, Good Luck, or simply a note to say Thinking of You, there's an envelope design for every occasion.

handmade envelopes

1 Take any rectangular piece of paper; gift-wrapping paper is ideal. Place the side of the paper that you would like to be on the outside of the finished envelope, facing down.

2 Fold the paper neatly across the middle, but not in half. Leave enough paper poking out from underneath to form your final envelope-sealing flap. For an A4 piece of printer paper, this is about 2 cm, for smaller sheets of paper, it should be in proportion to this, as illustrated.

3 Using a ballpoint pen, mark a straight line parallel to the two side edges, about the same distance in from each edge as the sealing flap is poking out. Press quite hard with the pen so that you crease through to the bottom bit of paper when you draw the line.

4 Cut the bottom corners off the folded paper to the line at about 60°. Cut the top corners from the top and the sides to meet at the drawn line, as illustrated, again at about 60°.

5 Unfold the paper so that the outside is facing upwards.

6 Carefully cutting with scissors or a craft knife and ruler, cut off the flaps on only half the paper to the lines you drew. Make sure you just cut the pen lines off with the flaps.

7 Turn the paper over and fold the remaining flaps over at the creases caused by pressing through with the ballpoint pen when you drew the lines earlier.

8 Apply glue or, better still, a thin strip of double-sided tape on each flap and peel off the backing.

9 Fold the paper over, taking care to make sure that it is square and that the edges line up nicely.

Make your letter a special one, too—when made from an A4 piece of paper, these envelopes will fit a paper shirt perfectly.

BIG-KITCHEN SCIENCE
Möbius strips

The *Möbius Strip* is a one-sided, one-edged loop named after an astronomer and mathematician called August Möbius. Making a Möbius strip is easy, and children aged six and up will be fascinated by this look into the world of *topology* and the science of the surface of a 3D shape. My dad first showed me how to make a Möbius strip, and I have never forgotten it or the profound impression the idea of a piece of paper only having one side made on me. Nor am I alone—scientists, mathematicians, engineers, and artists have all been fascinated by this weird form. There are some very interesting things to consider with a Möbius strip, and despite its simplicity as a project, it will get your kids thinking about how we describe forms and categorize shapes and surfaces.

It won't take you long to get started on this project. Soon you'll be able to cut two circular loops of paper along their lengths so that they turn into a square-edged frame before your very eyes—the nearest you're ever likely to get to being able to do magic.

Mind-bending adventures in topology

Kids love to categorize things; it helps them make sense of the world they are learning about as they grow up. It is mesmerizing to them that different 3D shapes can be put into similar groups based on how many surfaces or edges they have. Kids can pick this sort of stuff up quicker than the average grown-up, because they haven't yet become entrenched in their thinking, and they'll quickly grasp concepts like this one.

6 years +

10 minutes

Sheet of paper
Scissors
Sticky tape or glue

Cut a strip from the edge of a piece of plain paper.

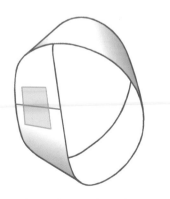

Make a cylindrical loop shape, then twist one end 180° (i.e., one-half turn) so that the ends line up.

Tape the ends together; that's it.

Once you have made your Möbius strip, you can do some cool things with it.

Try coloring it in; can you color both sides different colors?

Try cutting it in half lengthways; you'll find something very strange happens.

Stick a Möbius strip at right angles to a untwisted loop, then cut these in half lengthways. You'll get a square frame—weird or what?

Stick a Möbius strip at right angles to another Möbius strip with a twist in the opposite direction.

You'll get two linked hearts—sweet science!

Experimental discussion

When did MC Escher draw his famous Möbius Strip picture?

The artist MC Escher loved the idea of the Möbius Strip and used it as the basis for his drawing *Möbius Strip II (Red Ants)*, completed in 1963. In the picture, the red ants keep walking around the strip but can never find the other side of it.

How is the Möbius Strip used practically in industry?

The lifespan of conveyor belts is doubled through use of this concept, as the belt gets worn over its whole area and not just one side.

What is topology?

Topology is the branch of geometry that deals with the study of the surface of a 3D shape. In topology, shapes are grouped into similar forms that all have the same number of surfaces, and not necessarily by their actual shape. In topology, a coffee mug can be described as a form of *torus*, or doughnut, because although it looks completely different, the coffee mug and doughnut actually share the same type of surfaces, only in the mug one side of the doughnut has been dented in.

Where can I see a Möbius Strip?

Did you know that the world-wide symbol for recycling is, in fact, a Möbius Strip?

Encourage Your Kids to Read More Books

Reading is great for both you and your children and is a fantastic form of relaxation and escapism. Reading books helps your children develop their language skills, extend their vocabulary, and their understanding of the world. Your children's spelling and writing skills are also improved by regular reading.

Reading can be especially helpful to your children when they are going through difficult times in their lives, such as the separation of parents, starting a new school, the death of a loved one, bullying, or puberty. A good book gives them a mental place to go where the day-to-day worries aren't so ever-present; it gives them new people to meet and gets them involved in other people's stories. Reading develops your children's creativity. It's better than the television, because when children get involved in the book they are reading, they imagine the characters and scenes, which paint all kinds of wonderful images in their minds in a far more interactive and satisfying way than television can ever do. Reading encourages your children to be creative and think for themselves.

So, everyone knows how good reading is for their children, but how do you encourage them to read, or read more? Here are ten top tips to get you started and get your children reading books.

1 Fill your house with books

Give your kids their own bookshelves so they can start collecting and treasuring their own favorite stories.

2 Read to them

Set up a nightly routine by reading a story or chapter from a book at bedtime. Bedtime reading is a great routine to get into because it is a perfect relaxing bridge between the excitement of the day and sleep. It is also a special time for you to be together without the stresses and hassles of the day, a time when all is calm and you are just having fun together

However, don't restrict yourself to bedtimes; read to them whenever the opportunity presents itself. Read them funny or interesting stories from the newspaper when you find them; save and read out loud a funny or moving poem before you eat a meal together; get them to read their homework out loud to you when they have finished it.

3 Listen to audiobooks in the car on longer journeys

Audiobooks make every long journey an exciting adventure in itself. If the story is good and the narration is well done, the journey will flash by, and when you reach your destination, you may even find yourselves wanting to stay in the car to hear the end of the story. They can be expensive, but most stories will bear repeated listening, and the lending library also lend out audiobooks for free.

4 Don't be a book snob

Children are inspired to read by all kinds of different books—graphic novels, magazines, web blogs, manuals, science fiction, or teenage romance, for example. Let them get interested in reading in whatever form that it takes to start with. Once they get into the habit of reading, their minds will expand to take in a wider and wider choice of material over time as their friends introduce them to new books and ideas.

5 Talk though the story when you read it

Talk about the characters in the story. If it is a novel, then talking about the main character's motivations, asking what your children think the characters are going to do next, or what is going to happen in the story, adds weight to the experience of reading. Asking questions about the writer's style or the way the writer describes the scenes will help your children get the most out of the story and will help them in a very subtle (but powerful) way to improve their own written schoolwork and homework assignments. Discussing stories and listening to what your children have to say about the characters and the situations they encounter in the book will tell you a lot about what your children are thinking and help you understand them better.

6 On weekends or holidays, make a treat of getting magazines

Magazines have short articles about things your kids like—horses, cars, fashion, gossip, TV shows, toys, video games, and popular science, for example. If they really like a particular magazine, then consider buying a subscription to it for them as a birthday (or other special occasion) present or to reward a special success at school.

Give books as gifts

Take the trouble to go to the bookstore on the weekend or browse the secondhand bookstore for interesting titles and involve your children in choosing the best book as a gift for someone you both know. When giving a book, especially to your children, always write their name and the date and a short message in the book inside the cover or on the flyleaf. Then they'll always know it's theirs and that you think that it is a precious gift that you have chosen specially for them.

8 Get a poetry book and occasionally read them a poem

Poems are fabulous for evoking emotions and feelings. The best poems condense and capture descriptions of scenes or feelings in a very powerful way, bridging the gap between stories and songs. Inspire your children with poems, and they will remember lines from them, and the times you read to them, for the rest of their lives.

9 Choose material that they like

There is plenty of time to discover the classics. To start with, choose books that you know your children will like. Choose different books to read to them than those they are going to read themselves. When you read to them, you can pick books with exciting or thrilling stories that may have longer words in them than the ones they would choose for themselves. Always explain a word or phrase if you think that they don't understand it. Perhaps you have seen a film that you all liked; get the book that inspired the film and read that. If they are reading to themselves, a graphic novel or even a book is an excellent way to start reading a film story.

10 Have a word of the day

Reading is as much about exploring language and the way stories are told as it is about the stories themselves. Look on the web or in a dictionary and pick a word of the day that you can all learn together. The word you choose can be gross or exciting, different or funny, long or strange, but above all, make sure that it is useful in some way. Get everyone to make up a sentence with the new word in it and give a point or star for the best sentence. If they want, let your children each find and tell their favorite new word of the day. A good time to do this is at meal times when you are all together.

There are three stages of a man's life:
He believes in Santa Claus;
He doesn't believe in Santa Claus;
He is Santa Claus.

UNKNOWN

mini USB tiffany lamp PAGE 216

victorian domed display case PAGE 234

samurai sword PAGE 228

mini USB
tiffany lamp

Make this fabulous miniature USB Tiffany lamp from a bottle cap

12 years +

2 hours

3 x Small copper coins
Paintbrush end
Marker
Emery paper
Superglue
Low-cost, USB LED lamp
Glue-gun glue
Paper clip
Bottle cap
Glass paint
Stained-glass, black craft outline
Soldering iron

Tiffany lamps are those beautiful, colored-glass lamps originally made by Louis Comfort Tiffany at the beginning of the twentieth century. Original Tiffany lamps command huge prices at auction, but now you can make one for yourself from a bottle cap, three coins, and the metal end of an old paintbrush.

The shade is made from a small, clear or transluscent bottle cap. You can paint any art nouveau pattern on the outside, and all you need are some colored permanent markers in red, yellow, and green for the design and a black marker or embossing pen for outlining the pattern. The lamp glows wonderfully with the superbright LED, easily hacked from a very cheap mini USB PC light. The LED light is just perfect as a starting point for making your lamp and contains everything you'll need to make the light work properly: the LED with the correct resistor, a short length of wire, and the USB plug.

mini USB tiffany lamp

1 Take three small copper (or silver) coins of diminishing size and superglue them together so that they are centered with respect to each other, in a nice, neat pile.

4 The stem of the lamp is made from a small paintbrush ferrule. Carefully remove the bristles and then either pull out or drill out the handle using a small gauge drill bit. If the bristles are glued in firmly, then the only way to remove them will be to cut them off at the tip of the ferrule and drill them out as well. When drilling, hold the ferrule gently in a vice to avoid injury.

2 Using black spray paint or a permanent black marker, color the coins all over.

5 Once you have removed the handle and the bristles, you will have a nice, miniature, tapering metal tube. Using a pair of pliers or other metal object, bend up a small part of the end of the ferrule (this is to let the wire out once the ferrule has been stuck to the coins).

3 Using the finest sandpaper you have, or wet-and-dry emery paper, rub down the coins to remove the black from all the edges and the top of the uppermost coin.

6 To make the lampshade support, you will need one medium-sized paperclip. Carefully straighten out two of the loops as shown.

▶

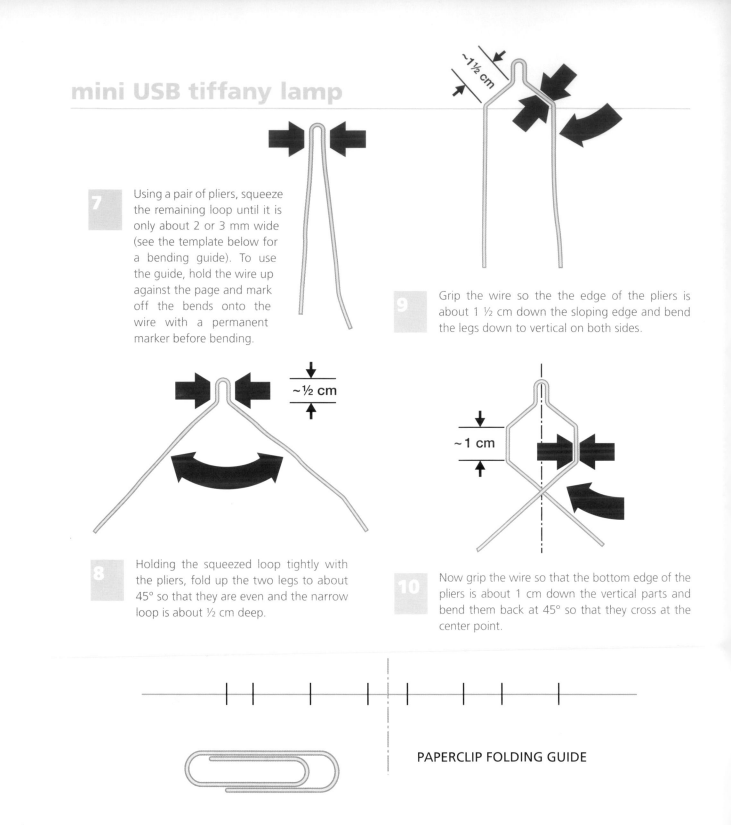

~1 ½ cm

7 Using a pair of pliers, squeeze the remaining loop until it is only about 2 or 3 mm wide (see the template below for a bending guide). To use the guide, hold the wire up against the page and mark off the bends onto the wire with a permanent marker before bending.

9 Grip the wire so the the edge of the pliers is about 1 ½ cm down the sloping edge and bend the legs down to vertical on both sides.

~½ cm

~1 cm

8 Holding the squeezed loop tightly with the pliers, fold up the two legs to about 45° so that they are even and the narrow loop is about ½ cm deep.

10 Now grip the wire so that the bottom edge of the pliers is about 1 cm down the vertical parts and bend them back at 45° so that they cross at the center point.

PAPERCLIP FOLDING GUIDE

~13mm

11 Finally, grip the wire so that the bottom edge of the pliers is about 13 mm down the sloping part and bend the legs back to the vertical so that they are level in the center.

12 Preparing the LED lamp is easy. Cut the USB plug off a standard (low-cost) USB laptop light. You will need strong pliers to cut through the spring and wire coating.

13 Remove the lens and slip out the LED.

14 Thread the LED wires through the ferrule and lay them so that they exit at the bottom of the tube, through the small gap you turned up earlier.

15 Carefully thread the paper-clip lampshade holder into the end of the ferrule and pull the LED down so that it sits in the middle of the wire shape, but does not short out on the metal parts.

quick-setting epoxy resin or glue-gun glue

16 Use quick-setting resin or glue-gun glue to seal up the base of the ferrule. If using glue-gun glue, then hold the ferrule with a tissue, because it is metal and will get hot when you squeeze the glue down inside it.

17 Use resin or superglue (cyanoacrylate) to glue the ferrule to the coin base. **DO NOT LET CHILDREN USE CYANOACRYLATE GLUE (SUPERGLUE).** Slip the lens back on to the LED to act as a diffuser.

18 To take the molded USB plug apart, carefully slit the rubbery plastic on one side and peel the plug molding off the inner metal part. Inside, the plug will have a metal case. Unfold the metal grips where the wire comes out of the plug and carefully remove the top part of the metal case.

RUBBERY OUTER

METAL CASE

19 Inside the metal case there will be more rubber. You must remove all the rubber carefully without damaging the plug. When removing the rubber, you will break the delicate wires that go to the 5 V and ground pins. Don't worry; you are going to solder new ones on, anyway.

PLASTIC PIN CHASSIS

TOP PART

20 Just to be sure, mark the plug pin that had the black wire coming from it using a permanent black marker.

SERIES A USB PLUG

| PIN 1 | 5 V |
| PIN 4 | GROUND |

21 When looking at the plug from the side that you are going to solder, the pins are arranged like this. Take care to get it right; you shouldn't be able to harm your computer, but if you get it around the wrong way, the LED will not light up.

glue-gun glue

22 When you have soldered the wires back on to the plug, get ready to replace the metal case top part. Put a small amount of glue-gun glue inside the plug to pot the wires nicely, and while the glue is still soft, clip the top case back on and bend the gripper around the neck of the metal case.

cyanoacrylate

glue-gun glue

23 Put some glue-gun glue around the wire end of the USB plug assembly and slip the rubber USB plug cover back around the metal case. Glue up using superglue. **NEVER LET CHILDREN USE CYANO-ACRYLATE (SUPERGLUE).**

24 A small, clear or transluscent bottle cap or personal healthcare product closure may be used for the lampshade. Drill a small (3 mm diameter) hole in the center of the top of the cap. Draw the stained-glass pattern onto the cap with a special tube of craft stained-glass liner (liquid lead).

26 Rest the lampshade on the lampshade holder. Glue it on if you like, or leave it unglued so that you can make a range of different lampshades.

25 Fill in the leaded-light-glass panels with transparent or glass paint. Use as many colors as you can to make a really bright and colorful lampshade.

Make the miniature lampshade from almost anything you like—paper, tracing paper, OHP film, or tissue. You could even make a Chinese lantern!

mini USB spotlight

Call Batman to your rescue with this fantastic working spotlight

12 years +	
2 hours	

Soldering iron
Glue gun
Superglue
Double-sided sticky tape
Silver paint

This project starts with a USB laptop light, which can be bought very cheaply online. A simple spotlight like this is the perfect way to start beginners soldering and making electrical circuits, but do take care as soldering irons get very hot and will give you a nasty burn if mishandled. Supervise children at all times; turn off the soldering iron immediately after use and do not leave any trailing flex. Part of this project also requires superglue and should therefore be done carefully by an adult.

I used a translucent cap from a cheap supermarket shampoo bottle, but any translucent round (barrel-shaped) cap will do. It is best to use translucent plastic because the real spotlight has heat dissipation vents at the side and these let some light out, which gives the spotlight those characteristic glowing rings.

When your light is finished, shine it upon to the wall, and you'll see you get an absolutely fantastic effect.

mini USB spotlight

1 For this project, you will need a small, translucent barrel. I used a cheap shampoo bottle closure.

2 Make the closure neat and round; cut off the flip-top lid it you need to. Coat some thick tin foil in double-sided sticky tape on one side, cut into five thin strips, and stick them evenly spaced round the cap.

3 Cut some shorter, slightly wider strips and stick these along the length of the barrel at 90° spacing.

4 Carve the power converter from a piece of wine bottle cork or something similar and cover with foil. Leave the side edges long so that they hide any poor joints.

5 Attach to the side of the barrel in line with what will become the bottom of the lamp.

6 Color in the top of the bottle lid. This will be the back end of the spotlight. Spray, paint, or use a silver pen to color it in. **DO NOT** color the sides between the strips.

▶

7 Cut the USB plug off the standard USB laptop light. You will need to use strong pliers to cut through the spring and wire coating.

8 Remove the light lens and slip out the LED.

glue-gun glue

glue-gun glue

9 Thread the LED wires through the lid and out through the hole that was in the top of the lid. Crumple some foil and glue in the base of the spotlight to act as a reflector, making sure that the wires aren't shorted onto it.

10 To take a molded-on plug apart, carefully slit the rubbery plastic on one side and peel the plug molding off the inner metal part. Inside, the plug will have a metal case. Unfold the metal grips where the wire comes out of the plug and carefully remove the top part of the metal case.

METAL CASE

RUBBERY OUTER

TOP PART

PLASTIC PIN CHASSIS

11 Inside the metal case there will be more rubber. You must remove all the rubber carefully without damaging the plug. When removing the rubber, you will break the delicate wires that go to the 5 V and ground pins. Don't worry; you are going to solder new ones on, anyway.

SERIES A USB PLUG

PIN 1 — 5 V

PIN 4 — GROUND

12 When looking at the plug from the side that you are going to solder, the pins are arranged like this. Take care to get it right; you shouldn't be able to harm your computer, but if you get it around the wrong way, the LED will not light up.

15 Place some transparent film over the top of the spotlight and mark a circle only slightly smaller than the inside diameter of the lamp. Mark three small tabs then cut out the lens with scissors.

glue-gun glue

13 When you have soldered the wires back onto the plug, get ready to replace the metal case top part. Put a small amount of glue-gun glue inside the plug to pot the wires nicely, and while the glue is still soft, clip the top case back on and bend the gripper around the neck of the metal case.

16 Mark out and then cut out the bat logo so that it is big enough to fit across the spotlight lens and then cut a strip of foil to line the inside of the spotlight.

cyanoacrylate

glue-gun glue

double-sided sticky tape

14 Put some glue-gun glue around the wire end of the USB plug assembly and slip the rubber USB plug cover back round the metal case. Glue up using superglue (cyanoacrylate). **NEVER LET CHILDREN USE CYANOACRYLATE (SUPERGLUE).**

17 Stick the bat logo to the front of the lens with double-sided sticky tape and fold the tabs down and put a small piece of double-sided sticky tape on each one. Do not peel off the backing.

▶

bat + yoke
TEMPLATES

18 Roll up the spotlight liner and put it into the spotlight. Peel the backing off one of the lens tabs and slip that one between the liner and the spotlight wall and stick in place. Repeat with the other tabs, making sure that the lens is level.

glue-gun glue

19 Cut some small, stiff cardboard rectangles and color in black with a permanent marker and glue-gun glue one to either side of the spotlight.

20 Fill the inside of a single-serving sport bottle top with old coins to give it some weight. Glue in with glue-gun glue.

mini USB spotlight

21 Fill with coins and glue-gun glue and before it sets, place right way up on some stiff cardboard and leave to set.

22 Using the templates and measuring against your spotlight diameter, mark out the shape of the yoke on a piece of thick, stiff cardboard, like foamcore.

23 Carefully cut out the yoke. To make this thick and strong, you may need to stick two or more pieces of cardboard together.

24 Glue the yoke into the single-serving bottle cap and spray or paint black.

25 Stick the spotlight in the yoke at the appropriate angle. The yoke will rotate using the drinking-cap mechanism, but if you want it to pitch as well, then secure to the yoke with pins or small nails.

glue-gun glue

The perfect way to start beginners soldering and making electrical circuits.

samurai sword

Making this wooden-bladed Samurai sword or *katana* will elevate you to the status of a legendary swordsmith

10 years +

90 minutes

3ft x 1in Plastic waste pipe
2 x 4cm Cupboard door knobs
13ft x 1cm Black webbing
Sink strainer
3ft Wood strip
Gold and color spray paint

A Samurai sword is a true work of art. The technique of making the blade by heating the metal up and cooling it down repeatedly was used to purify the metal, and the results, even in the thirteenth and fourteenth centuries with ancient forging equipment, were amazing. Modern swords are judged not to be as good as those made hundreds of years ago by the great Japanese swordsmiths. Samurai swords have become renowned for their sharpness and cutting ability, and even though the blade on our sword isn't metal, the smoothly finished hardwood does have a satisfyingly Japanese feel to it. And, of course, you wouldn't really want your kids running round with a high-carbon-steel sword so sharp it could dice concrete.

samurai sword

1 Because the paint will take some time to dry, the first thing you must do is prepare the pipe and paint it. The pipe is going to be the handle (TSUKA) and the scabbard (SAYA), so take about 3 feet of plastic waste pipe and cut it in two, roughly 30cm from one end. Make sure that the cut is at right angles to the length of the pipe and not on a slant.

2 Sandpaper the surface of the plastic pipe with a fine grade of sandpaper to rough up the surface and provide a key for the paint. Paint or spray the long part black, brown, or bright red. Spray down inside one end a little bit, because this will be the mouth of the scabbard. Spray the short part gold or silver. Use a bottle to hold the pipe while it dries.

3 Cut the sword blade (KEN) and tang (the bit that fits inside the handle) (NAGAGO) from a single strip of hardwood, such as oak or beech, 3 cm x 1 cm. Cut the wood so that it is a bit shorter than the plastic pipe bits together (about 92 cm). There is no need to make a dangerous point, just cut the corner off the end for an authentic look.

4 Sandpaper the wood with medium and then fine sandpaper to give a slightly rounded edge to the blade (KEN). Take care not to get splinters in your fingers as you rub the sandpaper up and down the blade. Only sandpaper the visible part of the blade.

▶

5 Hammer a small nail into the center of the end of the wooden strip at the handle end and glue the doorknob onto the end of the wood. This is only a temporary fixing to hold the doorknob steady while you do the next stage.

6 Mix up some car body or decorator's resin filler (two-part epoxy filler) and spread it neatly around the joint between the door- knob and the wood end. Quickly, and before the resin has set, slide the handle pipe part over the wood and up to the doorknob.

7 When the resin is in its rubbery pre-setting stage, trim off any bits that have squeezed out of the joint to make the joint between the doorknob and the pipe handle part neat and free of resin. Let the resin set hard (15 mins) before moving on to the next stage.

8 A sink plug strainer makes an ideal guard (TSUBA), and because you are using waste pipe to make the handle and scabbard, you'll find that a sink strainer should be a good fit with your handle.

9 Cut out a rectangular hole in the flat part of the strainer, the size of your blade. Most strainers these days are metal-plated plastic. If you have one of these, then all you will need is a pair of scissors to cut the hole. If you have a metal one, you will need tin snips and or a metal file.

10 To fix the handle and make it feel really solid, mix up some more two-part resin and neatly fill out the other end of the handle pipe around the wooden blade.

GLUE

samurai sword

 Before it sets, push the guard onto the blade and slide it down to rest on the top on the handle end.

Either using more of the two-part resin you have just mixed up or using some new resin, put a small amount around the end of the handle area over the inner part of the strainer guard so that the resin goes through the strainer holes and bonds to the resin that is packing out the end of the handle.

 Now it's time to fit the end cap to the scabbard. Using another doorknob, coat the end of the doorknob and the inside of the scabbard pipe in two-part resin.

14 Gently push the doorknob into the end of the scabbard pipe. Remove any excess resin

15 Quickly turn the pipe over so that the uncured resin doesn't run down inside the scabbard. Rest the doorknob on the floor and keep the scabbard vertical until the resin has set (usually 10 to 15 minutes, depending on how much hardener you used when mixing it up).

GLUE

16 To achieve that distinctive look that is normally made from carefully overlapping the braid (ITO), you are going to wrap the handle in a narrow webbing. Any color will do, but black looks really good. Start winding the webbing around the handle in a spiral, keeping the gaps between the webbing even and about half the width of the webbing apart. Lay a strip of glue under the webbing as you go and keep the webbing tight. This is a two-person job. Hot, melted (glue-gun) glue is the best for this. Seal any cut ends of the webbing with a lighted match to stop them fraying.

GLUE

18 The cord (SAGEO) was used to tie back clothing when the sword bearer was about to fight. Ninjas had longer cords and would use the cord to hold the sword in their teeth so as to keep both hands free for climbing. To make the cord, glue down some webbing and double it over itself and glue down again so that it looks like a bow.

GLUE

17 When you reach the end, go once around the handle completely to cover up the end of the handle and then start spiralling back up the handle. Take care to keep the space between the windings even and the same as the windings going the other way, so that the diamond shapes created by the counterwise wrapping are in a straight line.

GLUE

19 Fold over the webbing strip at 45° and wrap the webbing around the scabbard twice in the same place so that a bit of thickness builds up. Glue the webbing every half-turn.

GLUE

20 After the second wrap, on top of the bow, move the web across so that you can make another wrap next to the first (about one-strap's width apart). Wrap the webbing strap around twice again in the new spot to create a second thick band. Cut the webbing off and seal the end with a lit match (an adult must do this part) then glue down. Now sheath your sword and you are ready to play—carefully now.

Become a heroic samurai swordsmith in just 90 minutes!

victorian domed display case

An authentic-looking Victorian clear display dome made from an old bottle

10 years +

1 hour

Glue gun
Black paint
Christmas ornament
Large plastic soda bottle
Felt

When you make something beautiful or bring back a memento from a long adventure, nothing is better than displaying your prized possession as the centerpiece of a mantle-shelf arrangement. In Victorian times, elegant drawing rooms up and down the land would have been stuffed to the gills with all kinds of knickknacks, neatly laid out to cover almost every available surface.

This project is the perfect way to display all your most beautiful holiday trinkets and the things that you make. It will keep the dust off them and show them off in a really special way. The best bit is that it's a quick little project, and all you need is some cardboard, a Christmas bauble or something similar, and an empty, two-liter plastic drinks bottle.

Your kids will love this project, and as the dome isn't glued down, you can lift it off just like in a real display case, and change the object whenever you feel like it.

victorian domed display case

1 Take one 2-liter soda bottle and cut it halfway down near the bottom and at the top. Avoid scratching or marking the upper part of the bottle, which is going to be the with width of the dome. Remove any label adhesive residue with nail polish remover or cellulose thinners and then polish the dome with furniture polish.

2 Use a hacksaw to cut off the top and hold the top rather than the bottle.

3 Using the base part, draw a circle on a suitable piece of thick cardboard, taking care not to squeeze the plastic base into an oval. Cut the cardboard out so that it is the same diameter as the bottle.

4 Use a large yogurt cup or similarly tapering food cup for the product stand. Cut off to a suitable height so that the base fits easily inside the dome and cut a large hole in the upturned bottom.

5 Glue the plastic cup base centrally to the cardboard and fill with some screws glue-gun glued in position to give it weight.

▶

victorian domed display case

6 Cover with suitable fabric (velvet) by gluing fabric down in the middle and then pulling taut all around and gluing to the edge of the cardboard. When glue is dry, trim off flush with the base of the cardboard.

7 Cut a strip of cardboard about 1½ cm wide. Paint or spray it black and then glue it around the covered cardboard base so the bottom edge is flush with the base of the cardboard.

8 To cover up the cut top of the soda bottle, use a plastic Christmas tree decoration with a metalized finish, cut in half.

9 Stick the decoration to the top of the soda bottle dome to cover up the cut top. Remove the Christmas decoration loop, or if there is a hole in the top of the decoration, cover with a blob of glue-gun glue or a stick on craft gem.

Go back in time with this stylish glass dome—a classic way to present the things you've made.

victoriana tennis rackets

Practice low-passing shots over the sofa and volley to win in your own Center Court playing with this lovely project.

The scroll work is what makes a simple piece of cardboard not only look beautiful, but strong enough to bat a lightweight ball back and forth. You can print a beautiful template from our website, but once you see how to make the rackets, why not design your own scroll work? As long as you make sure that there are a few strips that go from the handle up and across the racket face, you can make the design anything you want: a butterfly, a shamrock, a love heart, or your national flag! The list is endless.

The project also shows you how to make a pompom ball from a piece of cardboard and a couple of plastic grocery bags. The resulting ball is resilient enough to bat about as hard as you like, and yet soft enough to play with indoors.

Become a world champion on grass or carpet with these gorgeous, gilded tennis rackets

8 years +

2 hours

Cardboard
Felt
grocery bag
Clear plastic sheet

download available

victoriana tennis rackets

1 Download the racket template from our website or draw your own design. Stick it onto some thick, corrugated cardboard using white glue and carefully cut it out.

2 Accurately cut some strips of thinner corrugated or lightweight cardboard. If you use corrugated, make sure to cut the strips across the flutes (not along them).

3 Curl up the end of a strip by wrapping it tightly around your finger.

4 Ideally using glue-gun glue (but white glue will work, too), glue one edge of the strip and stick it onto the racket pattern so that it follows one of the curving lines.

5 Repeat for all the strips. For more complex shapes, fold up the shape and pinch it together so you can apply the glue more easily to its edge.

6 Carefully glue all the strips onto the rackets to follow all the lines.

victoriana tennis rackets

7 Either follow the pattern or add bits into the pattern to make it more intricate if you want.

8 When you have stuck strips over all the lines, spray or paint the racket all over. You can use any color, but silver or gold look really nice and give the effect of gilded, wrought metalwork.

9 Carefully apply glue to the top edge of the strips and cover the racket with a thin sheet of clear plastic from some old packaging, or an overhead projector slide.

10 Carefully draw the shape of the racket onto the plastic layer using a permanent marker, then cut out around the edge using strong scissors.

11 Neatly draw over the glued cardboard edge using a gold or silver marker. This hides the glued edge and makes the scroll work look much neater.

▶

victoriana tennis rackets

12 Cut a strip of felt, material, or leather the same thickness as the racket and glue around the edge. Glue it to the outer bulges of the scroll-work swirls.

13 Repeat for the other racket. Use a different design for the scroll work if you want, or a contrasting color for the edge strip material.

x2

14 Trace the pompom disc templates from page 40 and stick them to a stiff piece of thin cardboard. Cut around the circle and cut out the hole in the middle.

16 Keep wrapping it around until you can't poke it through the hole in the middle. Use more than one carrier bag if you need to.

15 Cut a thin plastic garbage bag in half lengthways and hold the two discs together, then wrap the plastic around the discs by poking it through the hole repeatedly. Make sure you wrap it nice and tightly.

17 Start with a knife if you have to, but then using strong, sharp scissors, cut around the edge of the wrapped disc. Poke the scissors in-between the two cardboard discs.

18 Use a length of plastic bag doubled over, or some string, and passing it between the discs, tie off as tightly as possible.

19 Trim off the ties and then trim the pompom to make sure it is as round as possible. Don't pull out any straggling bits of plastic, just trim them off.

20 You're all ready to play. Because the ball is nice and soft, this game is safe to play indoors or outdoors.

While away any rain-stopped-play afternoons during Wimbledon!

gel cell battery

Make a real battery that will power a clock from stuff that you find around the kitchen

12 years +

2–3 hours

Empty 35mm-film containers
Salt
Vinegar
Gelatin (or fruit jelly)
Absorbent paper
Copper wire
Aluminium cooking foil
Kitchen scissors
Craft knife
Pliers

download available

This experiment involves mixing salt, vinegar, and jelly. It's satisfyingly challenging, but certainly not beyond any older child/dad team. The effort is well worth it, and unlike the typical wet-cell, homemade battery, this design is really compact and looks and works just like the real thing. The experiment can be used as a basis for some interesting discussions about the mechanism of electricity generation.

We made four cells so that we could get a mechanical clock working; however, if you only want to make one or two cells, you might try using them to power a simple low-power LCD clock. Our website has printable labels so that you can make your batteries look just like the real thing!

gel cell battery

1. Strip about 6½ ft of multistrand copper wire.

x 6½ ft

2. Cut out 12 strips of aluminium baking foil approximately 2½cm x 30cm.

x 4

3. Lay the foil strips in four piles of three pieces and twist together about 30 mm of one end and fold the twisted part out at right angles.

4. Cut out four strips of blotting paper, or absorbent kitchen paper towel, approx 4cm x 1½ft.

5. Make a mark on the paper at the halfway point. Then on one half, carefully lay out a 1½ft length of the bared copper strands, doubling it back and tacking it lightly at each end with a spot of glue-gun glue. Twist together about 3cm at the end of the wire and bend out at right angles to the paper. The paper part is called the separator and stops the two electrodes touching and making a short circuit.

6. Fold the paper separator over to cover the copper wire.

7. Lay one of the aluminium piles on top of the paper.

▶

gel cell battery

x 4

8 Roll up the sandwich taking care to make sure that no strands of copper poke out. If they do, tuck them back in. thev must not touch the aluminium

9 Secure the roll with a small piece of sticky tape.

Your completed cell roll should look like this:

11 Use an old 35mm-film film tub for the battery casing, or cut and roll up a toilet paper tube and seal one end with a slice off a wine bottle cork (seal with glue-gun glue).

12 Put the rolled-up cell in the casing.

10 GEL ELECTROLYTE RECIPE:

3 teaspoons gelatin
(or pack, 135g, of fruit jelly)
1 tablespoon salt
2 tablespoons vinegar
150ml tap water

Make up about 150ml of jelly. Put jelly or gelatin with vinegar and heat in the microwave on high for 10 seconds and stir, then add 150ml of cold water.

13 Cut a rectangular hole in the film tub cap big enough for the copper wire and aluminum-twisted end to poke through.

14 Carefully and slowly pour the gel electrolyte mix into the middle of the rolled-up battery cell. Do not fill to the brim as the mix will bubble as a reaction starts at each electrode. As the bubbles form, the cell will float up a little. Leave for about 20 minutes, then gently push the cell down and top up with a tiny bit of the electrolyte mix.

15 Carefully put the cap on the tub so that the electrodes poke out of it and are not touching. This cell will generate between about 0.5 V and 0.6 V. This is not a very strong battery and will not produce more than about 3mA or 4mA. Connect the batteries together in series (i.e., connect the positive of one battery to the negative of another) using three strands of copper wire twisted together and tied in a granny knot around the electrodes.

16 Trace and cut out the two template battery and holder shapes. The cross bar of the T is correctly sized for either an AA or an AAA battery.

battery TEMPLATES

gel cell battery

17 Stick the templates to a piece of stiff, thick cardboard (corrugated cardboard is good or foamboard if you have it).

18 Make two small holes in the top edge and glue-gun glue a piece of copper wire into each hole.

19 Bend the wires around the edge of the cardboard and glue-gun glue to secure on the back edge.

20 Connect to output wires of your battery array by twisting the wires together (to the correct polarity).

21 Now you can test your battery as a replacement for any 1.5 V single cell.

22 Four batteries will be enough to replace an AA or AAA 1.5 V battery in most low-drain applications (LCD clock or MP3 player). Your battery might only run for a few minutes or a few days, but then it didn't cost $20 m to develop! If you want a stronger battery, look on the web and experiment with the electrode materials.

In 1831, Michael Faraday built the first electric dynamo—a simple form of generator—and showed that electricity could be generated mechanically rather than just chemically.

BIG-KITCHEN SCIENCE
Seed growing

And they're off! A broad bean is the ideal starting point for a seed-growing experiment. Big and full of all the stuff a plant needs to get growing quickly, beans are often used in schools to teach students about germination and what happens when a dormant seed starts to grow into a new plant. This experiment is a neat twist on that time-honored tradition, because by growing the beans down into water in clear tubes (instead of in soil) you can watch the progress of the roots as they develop. Even better, you can line up your beans and race them against each other.

Growing a plant from a seed is a great experimental project because there's something weirdly magical about it, and yet it is really proper science. On page 250, you can see what the beans look like after one week. The bean at the far end had seven drops of a liquid plant food, and the bean in the middle had only one drop, but was accidentally put into the tube upside down (with respect to the growing shoot) so the leaves are trying to grow down into the water. The nearest bean had no drops of liquid feed at all and is growing in plain water.

Ready, steady, grow.

To avoid disappointment, the beans are presoaked, and more beans than you need for the experiment are pregerminated in a special little incubator. This is a long-term project. Once set up in their tubes, the beans will continue to grow for weeks, so your children can keep coming back to check progress. To make it even more scientific, why not selectively add a few drops of plant nutrient to the tubes or grow different kinds of beans in each tube?

6 years +
1 month

Clear poly-tubing
Cardboard
Broad beans
Craft knife
Sealable container
Dressmaker's pins
Marker

Put some nice, big, fat, broad beans in a bowl of water and leave for 24 hours.

 Roughly cut out a cardboard strip, cut some holes in it that just fit the beans, and gently poke the beans into it, so that they are all standing up.

Put a wet kitchen towel into the bottom of a sealable plastic box, place the beans and cardboard support in the box, close the lid, and put it somewhere warm and light. Inspect the beans every day until shoots appear.

While you are waiting for the shoots to appear, make the racetrack. Get some clear poly-tubing with an internal diameter just a little bit bigger than the width of the beans. Broad beans are big, so you'll probably need the biggest, clear tubing you can get (I used 19 mm diameter tubing). Cut tubing into three same-sized lengths, about 1½ft long.

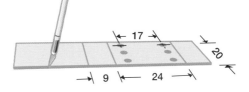

Make the tubing holder from a single wide strip of cardboard folded around, or separate pieces glue-gun glued together. For 19mm tubing, the box needs to be at least 9cm high, and the holes need to be about 17cm apart, to allow the tubing to bend around easily. If you want to paint the cardboard, paint it now, before you assemble the rest of the experiment.

 Poke the tubing through the holes and arrange in neat, semicircular curves.

7 Crease and then fold the box section a around under the tubes and glue permanently.

8 To stop the beans falling down the tubes, push a dressmaker's pin through each tube wall, all the way through one wall and partially into the other opposite one, about three-quarters of a bean-length down the length of tubing. When your beans have started to sprout, take them out of their incubator and gently place one in the end of each tube resting on the pin.

9 Carefully fill the tubes up with water to just below the dressmaker's needles. To follow the growth of the bean root, mark the tubes with ballpoint pen or permanent marker each day. You'll be amazed at how fast they grow. Choose one bean each at the beginning of the race, and see whose bean wins.

Experimental discussion

? Which bit of the seed grows first?

The root starts to grow first. This anchors the plant in the ground and enables it to start drawing up water. As it lengthens, it lifts the first leaves clear of the ground so that they can start catching the sunlight as soon as possible. The first tip that appears is called the *radicle*, the main part that then extends is called the *hypocotyl*.

? Where does the plant come from?

A huge oak tree grows from a tiny acorn, so where does all that mass come from? It doesn't come from the soil, that's for sure! Apart from a few nutrients, the roots only bring water into the tree. The tree actually builds itself from air using sunlight as a power source. The solid part of the tree (the bit that isn't water) is made by the tree using a process called *photosynthesis*, where the tree uses sunlight to unlock the carbon from carbon dioxide gas in the air.

? How much does a big tree weigh?

A large, mature beech tree 100ft tall, with a trunk diameter of 1ft, weighs about 9 tons, 8 tons of which are above ground. The biggest giant redwood trees can weigh as much as 2,500 tons.

BEING THERE

Start your kids collecting as a hobby

Collecting bugs, rocks, leaves, baseball cards, stamps, coins, Barbie dolls, or in fact anything, is a part of childhood. Of course, it can be a big part of adulthood, too. So do you have a collecting passion you would like to share with your children? Or would you just like to spend some really high-quality time with them over a longer-term project that you can both learn about and get enthusiastic over?

As parents, we all have an innate desire to teach our children, to give them the tools to survive and prosper in the world as they grow up. Collecting is a wonderfully pain-free way to learn about the world together while having fun.

1 Be creative and start your children off on their collection

If your child hasn't already started a collection, you can start them off; it's a great shared activity. Pick something that you both like, or more importantly, something that you know they will like, and that you can become interested in. Suggest it to them and perhaps give them a few examples.

Finding out about things and putting them in order is fun, almost with whatever you are collecting. Be as creative and original as you can. Of course, the collection might be action figures or crystals, but it could just as easily be hair ties, matchboxes, or shrunken potato chip bags, paper clips, or rubber bands.

You could start the collection as a summer project, and if they are young, steer them towards something simple and easy to collect, with the target of the collection being to put all the things in rows in a nice display box frame to hang on the wall, for example, by the end of the summer. You never know; this little project may go on to be a life-long passion of theirs.

2 Consider the opportunities for learning

Consider the link between collecting and any educational elements of the collection, i.e., stamp collecting and geography or history, or game-card collecting and cultural influences, for example. Collecting is part of a strong, built-in desire in all of us to categorize and organize our experiences and learning so that we can make sense of the world. Take time to consider how your children's collections can increase their knowledge of more than just the collection itself.

3 Consider the opportunities for their personal development

Collecting anything, and finding out about it, develops a whole range of important life skills that we will carry through to adulthood. It is a discipline with brief and often clearly defined parameters: the collection provides a framework, it teaches presentation skills, it promotes the pride of ownership that extends beyond the mere cost of an object, and teaches children to plan and consider what they need to do to achieve their goals.

4 Learn facts about the collection

Learn the basics about what your child is collecting. For example, if your child is collecting Pokémon figurines (or cards), take the time to learn the names and special powers of a few of the important creatures, or learn the basic game strategies. This will help you appreciate what your children like about their collection and what parts of it are important to them. In a wider sense, get interested in what they are interested in; often getting interested in something is all about understanding it more, and once you are on their wavelength, you'll understand them more and have some more shared experiences.

Note: Commercial products designed to collect are not necessarily the most fun or the best value for a special collection or a collecting project that you can both share.

Don't take over

Remember this is your child's collection, help your child and be involved but don't start a better collection and become competitive. It would be all too easy with your age and resources to be able to quickly build a better collection; all this will do is discourage the child. Let them have something which is truly their own.

Don't overindulge your child

Collecting is all about slowly building up a collection of related things, each with its own special story and providence. It's much too easy to go out and buy all the latest objects, but there is little reward in that, and the resulting collection will have little meaning.

Make the hunt or bargain-hunting part of the thrill of collecting. The best collections are those that take time to build up and where there is a rewarding and interesting story to be told about each item in the collection. Use eBay, yard sales, or scour second- hand and charity shops. Remember, life is as much about enjoying the moment. The search should be as exciting as the acquisition and can become a great shared pastime.

Don't allow it to become an obsession

Kids tend to obsess about things in general and they can become obsessive collectors. Obsession is something that we should grow out of by the time we are adults, otherwise it can have a damaging effect on our lives.

Don't become obsessed with the collection yourself. Even though you have fun working on the collection together, make sure that you don't make everything you do somehow related to the collection, otherwise your children might quickly become sick of it.

Help make something for the collection

Make and decorate a scrapbook, a box for the game cards, make an index file, a filing system on the computer, design a simple web page for the collection so that you can share the findings with others, or build a box frame or display case for the collection. This will build other skills and guard against the obsession becoming too one-track focused.

Supply reference material on the collecting subject

Supply materials and reference materials to enable the collecting and increase the knowledge about the collection or the background of the collectables. Look out for books on the subject (i.e., rocks or crystals, seeds, bugs, photography) in secondhand stores or the local charity shops, for example.

Put on a collection show

Get your children to put on a show of their collection. Organize this for friends and family or just you and your child's brothers and sisters. Better still, suggest that they do a presentation at school for their class. Help them in organizing this by suggesting it to their teacher. Most schools have a time each week, or at least once a semester, for children to do a "show and tell." This is a great opportunity for them to show off their passion and demonstrate their wider knowledge of their special subject. Help them prepare, and if they are presenting at school, make sure they practice their presentation in front of you first.

Epilogue

1. Sand castle maker
2. Satellite antenna dish
3. Shower head (holes drilled in bottom)
4. Measuring device (volume or length)
5. Garden pot
6. Horse feeder
7. Musical instrument (drum)
8. Fish tank
9. Door stop
10. Circle guide
11. Weapon
12. Robot head
13. Color sample
14. Birthday present
15. Tent peg mallet
16. Tortoise house
17. Pastry roller
18. Echo chamber
19. Small table
20. Giant's earring
21. Toilet
22. Infant's chair
23. Hazard marker
24. Kindling (chop up a wooden bucket)
25. Lampshade

So how many thinking-outside-the-box uses did you come up with for a bucket? Here are my twenty-five. I bet you can think of loads more...

Have fun being with your children, making the most of the time you spend together and thinking outside-the-box in a new way, every day.